AMAZON RIVER CRUISE
TRAVEL GUIDE 2025

Comprehensive Guide To Exploring Rain Forest Scenic Wonders, Top Destinations, Diverse Flora and Fauna, Outdoor Adventures With the Best Insider Recommendations.

GLOBAL
DESTINATIONS
CARAWAY TRAVELS

RICHARD CARAWAY

Disclaimer.

The information contained in this book is for general information purposes only. The author and publisher have made every effort to ensure the accuracy of the information provided, but make no guarantees or warranties of any kind, express or implied, about the completeness, accuracy, reliability, suitability, or availability of the information and resources contained herein.

This book is intended to provide helpful and informative content to readers, but it should not be relied upon as a substitute for professional advice. The author and publisher are not responsible for any errors or omissions, or for the results obtained from the use of this information.

Readers are advised to verify any information contained in this book with other reliable sources and to exercise their own judgment when planning and booking travel arrangements. The author and publisher shall not be liable for any losses, injuries, or damages from the display or use of this information.

Contents

CHAPTER 1.

BEFORE YOU GO: ESSENTIAL PREPARATIONS

Welcome to Beautiful Amazon River Cruise

The Amazon River, revered as the world's largest river by volume, is an epic journey through the heart of the Earth's most biodiverse region. Known to many as "the River Sea," its waters flow across a 4,000-mile expanse, cutting through multiple countries and creating a life-giving vein for the Amazon Rainforest—a place often called "the lungs of the Earth." More than just a river, the Amazon is a thriving ecosystem and cultural stronghold, where natural beauty and human history converge to create a world of unparalleled wonder and complexity.

An Amazon River cruise immerses guests in a vibrant and ancient environment that feels almost mythical. These waters are home to an amazing variety of wildlife, from pink river dolphins gliding gracefully through the currents to elusive jaguars prowling the riverbanks. Parrots and macaws fly through the trees in bright colours, while caimans and capybaras quietly patrol the shores. The Amazon is a living example of life's incredible diversity, with more plant and animal species than almost anywhere else on the planet. Each cruise day brings something new and exciting: an unexpected animal sighting, a hidden lagoon, or a glimpse into life in the nearby riverside villages.

But the Amazon is known for more than just its natural wonders; it is also a land of deep cultural significance. For centuries, indigenous tribes have called these waters home, their lives shaped by the river's cycles and their traditions deeply ingrained in the land. A journey down the Amazon is as much a cultural experience as it is a wilderness adventure. You will be drawn into a tapestry of customs, languages, and beliefs passed down through many generations. Encounters with local communities provide insight into a way of life that balances a deep respect for nature with a sustainable approach to survival—values that are relevant in today's global discussion about environmental stewardship.

Beyond its biodiversity and cultural wealth, the Amazon River captivates with its sheer size and beauty. Imagine waking up every morning to the gentle movement of the river and the chorus of jungle life greeting you. Mist rises from the water's surface, casting an otherworldly glow over the landscape as the day unfolds with new possibilities. Every bend in the river reveals a new breathtaking scene: towering trees, hidden coves, and seemingly endless green extending as far as the eye can see. It's a place where time slows down, where simply observing becomes a meditation, and where nature's rhythms invite you to abandon the hectic pace of modern life.

One of the Amazon's most intriguing features is the "Meeting of the Waters," a natural phenomenon near Manaus, Brazil. The dark waters of the Rio Negro and the sandy-hued Solimões River flow side by side for miles without fully mixing due to temperature, speed, and density differences. This striking border between two rivers is more than just a visual treat; it serves as a powerful reminder of the Amazon's complexity and mystery, a place where scientific wonders coexist with ancient legends.

Each Amazon River cruise is a combination of exploration and discovery, tailored to the diverse interests of passengers. While luxury ships provide amenities that make the experience smooth and indulgent, smaller eco-cruises offer intimate, immersive encounters with the jungle's raw beauty. Regardless of your travel style, the Amazon rewards curiosity and open-heartedness. Guided excursions frequently take you off the boat and into the rainforest, where naturalists and local guides share their knowledge of the plants and animals. Nighttime boat tours show you the nocturnal side of the river, where the forest comes alive with the sounds of frogs, insects, and distant animal calls, reminding you of how alive the Amazon truly is.

An Amazon River cruise is more than just a scenic journey; it is also transformative. For many, the experience instills a renewed appreciation for nature's intricate balance and humanity's place within it. The Amazon challenges you to look beyond the familiar and embrace the unknown. It serves as a reminder of how small we are in the grand scheme of things— and how much we still have to learn from nature. Travellers frequently leave with feelings of reverence and awe, a better understanding of the

Amazon's role in our global ecosystem, and a personal connection to a region that appears both timeless and fragile.

Setting foot on an Amazon River cruise is to embark on a journey of respect and admiration for one of the world's last great wildernesses. You'll see not only the beauty of the rainforest, but also the resilience of the people who live there, each of whom adds to the region's long history. Every twist in the river, every encounter with its wildlife, and every sunset casting a golden glow over the water serve as reminders that the Amazon is more than just a place to visit; it's an invitation to connect, learn, and grow. Welcome to the journey of a lifetime.

Geographical Overview and Unique Features

The Amazon River stretches over 4,000 miles, winding its way across the South American continent from the Andes in Peru to the Atlantic coast of Brazil. It is a river of superlatives, not only the world's largest by volume but also one of the longest, rivaling the Nile in length. The Amazon Basin, which spans around 2.7 million square miles, is the largest drainage basin on Earth, covering vast portions of Brazil, Peru, Colombia, and portions of other countries, including Bolivia, Ecuador, Venezuela, and Guyana. This immense area holds more than half of the world's remaining rainforest, representing an ecosystem so rich that scientists are still discovering new species here every year.

The Amazon River is both vast and dynamic, with seasonal variations that alter the landscape. During the high-water season, which runs from December to May, the river swells significantly due to rainfall and snowmelt from the Andes, forming a network of interconnected waterways that extends into the rainforest. In some areas, the river can stretch up to 25 miles wide, covering forested areas and allowing fish and other aquatic species to move freely among the trees. This seasonal flooding nourishes the soil, adding to the Amazon's incredible biodiversity. During the low-water season, which runs from June to November, the river recedes, exposing sandy beaches and providing access to trails and more remote areas of the rainforest.

The "Meeting of the Waters" near Manaus, Brazil, is one of the Amazon's most breathtaking natural wonders. Here, the dark, acidic waters of the Rio Negro converge with the sandy, sediment-laden Solimões River. For miles, the two rivers flow side by side without mixing, creating a stunning visual contrast that attracts both visitors and scientists. This phenomenon is caused by differences in river temperature, speed, and density, and the stark contrast between black and brown waters serves as a powerful reminder of the Amazon's complexity and the unique forces that shape its environment.

The Amazon River's vast network of tributaries, which number approximately 1,100 in total, adds to its grandeur. Over a dozen of these are "white-water" rivers, carrying silt and sediments from the Andes, while others are "black-water" rivers, such as the Rio Negro, which appear darker due to organic materials on the forest floor. These tributaries enrich and diversify the ecosystem by supporting species that have evolved to thrive in these diverse aquatic environments. Together, they form a vast, interconnected network that serves as the rainforest's lifeblood.

Rio Negro River

The geographical features of the Amazon Basin contribute directly to its ecological diversity. It has a diverse range of ecosystems, including rainforests, floodplain forests, and savannahs, each with its own flora and fauna. This region contains over 390 billion individual trees from thousands of species, forming a dense canopy that filters sunlight to the ground below. This layered structure creates distinct habitats at different levels: the emergent layer with towering trees, the dense canopy that houses the majority of the rainforest's wildlife, the understory that shelters a variety of birds and insects, and the forest floor, a shadowed, humid world teeming with life. This vertical diversity within the rainforest is what accounts for the Amazon's abundance of species, ranging from tiny insects to large mammals.

The Amazon's significance extends well beyond its immediate surroundings. The rainforest acts as a global climate regulator, storing

16

massive amounts of carbon and generating approximately 20% of the world's oxygen. It influences weather patterns not only in South America, but all over the world, as moisture released by its trees rises into the atmosphere and contributes to rainfall across the continent. This water cycle is so powerful that scientists believe deforestation in the Amazon could affect rain patterns as far as North America.

The Amazon River is also home to a diverse range of wildlife, many of which have adapted to its fluctuating water levels. Pink river dolphins, one of the Amazon's most iconic species, have evolved to navigate flooded forests, while giant otters, manatees, and a variety of catfish thrive in these intricate aquatic environments. The river's fish population alone is enormous, with over 3,000 known species and many more yet to be discovered. The Amazon is a birdwatcher's paradise, with colourful species such as macaws, toucans, and hoatzins flitting through the treetops and harpy eagles soaring overhead.

Amazon Pink river dolphin

Travellers to the Amazon are frequently captivated by the vastness of its waters and the endless horizon of green. From the river, you can see the rainforest's towering walls, hear the calls of unseen creatures, and feel the humidity in the air. Each turn in the river reveals something new, such as a hidden cove, a bustling riverbank, or a stretch of forest that appears to have remained unchanged by time. Exploring the Amazon is an exercise in perspective; the vastness of the river and the dense, layered ecosystem serve as reminders of nature's enduring power and mystery.

With all of its beauty and complexity, the Amazon River is a world unto itself. Its geographical features create an environment so distinct that visiting feels like entering another world—one in which water, land, and life are inextricably linked. For those fortunate enough to take an Amazon River cruise, it is more than just a journey across a river; it is an immersion into one of the world's most breathtaking natural spectacles.

A Brief History and Rich Culture

The Amazon River is as rich in history and culture as it is in biodiversity. Its story begins thousands of years ago, long before European explorers laid eyes on its vast waters. Indigenous peoples have inhabited the Amazon Basin for at least 11,000 years, developing complex societies that adapted to the rhythms of the river and forest. The Amazon has been a cradle of life, sustenance, and spiritual significance for its native inhabitants—a source of resources and a home for diverse tribes whose identities are intertwined with the land.

The indigenous communities of the Amazon, such as the Yanomami, Kayapo, and Ashaninka, have developed a thorough understanding of their surroundings. Their lives are shaped by a deep understanding of the Amazon's natural cycles, and they regard the forest and river as living beings worthy of respect and reverence. These tribes have developed sophisticated techniques for sustainable farming, hunting, and fishing, which ensures that their lifestyles are environmentally friendly. For example, "terra preta," or "dark earth," is a unique type of nutrient-rich soil created by ancient Amazonians using a combination of charcoal, plant matter, and other organic materials that is still present today as proof of their sustainable agricultural practices.

When Spanish and Portuguese explorers arrived in the 16th century, they were astounded by the size of the Amazon River and the forest's impassable vastness. Francisco de Orellana, a Spanish conquistador, was the first European to travel the entire length of the Amazon in 1542. His journey was fraught with difficulties, including clashes with indigenous warriors, whom he described as fierce and well-organized. These encounters sparked legends that Orellana had met warrior women resembling the Amazons of Greek mythology, hence the name "Amazon River." Early European accounts of the region were frequently fantastical, reflecting the explorers' amazement and the region's mystique.

The Amazon was largely ignored by colonial powers for centuries due to its remote location and difficult terrain. The river did not receive much attention from the outside world until the nineteenth century, when the rubber boom fueled its popularity. Demand for rubber increased dramatically in Europe and North America, and Amazon became the world's primary supplier. The rubber boom brought enormous wealth to the region, but it also caused exploitation and suffering among indigenous communities. Rubber barons established vast plantations, frequently forcing indigenous people to work and disrupting their way of life. Cities like Manaus in Brazil grew rapidly, and Manaus' Teatro Amazonas—a stunning opera house in the heart of the rainforest—stands as a relic of this era, symbolizing the wealth and opulence that rubber brought to a few at the expense of many others.

With the decline of the rubber industry in the early twentieth century, the Amazon region faced a new set of challenges as development projects like logging, agriculture, and mining began to reshape the landscape. These industries have had a significant impact on the Amazon's ecology and indigenous cultures, frequently causing deforestation and community displacement. Despite these pressures, many indigenous groups have survived, preserving their traditions, languages, and ties to the land. Their resilience demonstrates the strength of their culture, which has withstood centuries of external influence and environmental change.

Today, the Amazon combines ancient traditions with modern challenges. Indigenous communities continue to practice ancestor-honoring customs, including ceremonies, dances, and songs passed down through generations. While some groups maintain traditional ways of life, others have adapted to incorporate elements of the modern world, frequently combining the old and new in novel ways. Many indigenous people are now involved in ecotourism, guiding visitors through the rainforest and sharing knowledge of medicinal plants, wildlife, and survival skills. This engagement provides travellers with a unique opportunity to learn about the wisdom and spirituality that underpin Amazonian life, as well as a source of income to help sustain communities.

The Amazon also has a vibrant non-indigenous culture shaped by a combination of European, African, and indigenous influences. This blend is most evident in Amazonian cuisine, music, and art. Brazil's traditional cuisine incorporates local ingredients such as açaí, cassava, and river fish, while music and dance reflect the country's cultural diversity. Amazonian culture also relies heavily on folklore and oral traditions. Stories about forest spirits, river dolphins that transform into humans, and other supernatural beings serve as warnings and expressions of the people's reverence for the forest's mysteries.

In recent decades, there has been a growing global recognition of the Amazon's cultural and ecological significance, prompting conservation efforts that include indigenous communities as key stakeholders. Organizations and governments are recognizing that protecting the Amazon requires both the preservation of its natural resources and the respect for its people's rights and knowledge. Indigenous voices are becoming more prominent in these efforts, advocating for sustainable practices and policies that respect their relationship with the land.

Visitors to the Amazon today have a unique opportunity to witness a region where history, culture, and nature coexist. The indigenous guides, storytellers, and artisans you meet are stewards of a world that has endured for millenniums. As they share their traditions and stories, visitors gain a better understanding of the Amazon's cultural diversity and resilience. In many ways, visiting the Amazon is a journey through time, revealing how ancient knowledge and modern challenges shape a place that is still considered one of the world's last true frontiers.

Understanding the Ecosystem and Biodiversity

The Amazon River and its surrounding rainforest represent one of the most complex and vibrant ecosystems on Earth. Stretching across roughly 2.7 million square miles, the Amazon Basin is home to an estimated 10% of the planet's known species, making it an unmatched biodiversity hotspot. This ecosystem is often called the "lungs of the Earth" due to its immense capacity to produce oxygen and absorb carbon dioxide, playing a critical role in regulating the global climate. Every corner of the Amazon is teeming with life—from the dense forest canopy and towering trees to the river's depths and the lush forest floor, creating a symbiotic environment where every species, large and small, plays a part in sustaining this natural wonder.

At the heart of the Amazon's ecosystem are its rivers, tributaries, and seasonal floodplains, which provide essential resources for countless species. The Amazon River itself supports over 3,000 species of fish, with new discoveries still being made. Some of these species are truly unique, like the famed pink river dolphin, which is known for its intelligence and striking color. The waters also host the giant Amazonian manatee, electric eels, and the fearsome piranhas, whose reputation often overshadows their crucial role in keeping the aquatic ecosystem balanced. These waters aren't just a habitat but a lifeline that nourishes the surrounding rainforest and the countless life forms that depend on its seasonal rhythms.

The Amazon's terrestrial ecosystem is equally mesmerizing, hosting an unparalleled diversity of plant and animal species. Its rainforest canopy, reaching heights of up to 200 feet, forms a dense, multi-layered shelter that sustains life at every level. The emergent layer, composed of the tallest trees, towers over the canopy, absorbing the most sunlight and housing birds like harpy eagles, which prey on monkeys and sloths. Beneath this lies the main canopy, a vibrant habitat for countless species, from colorful macaws and parrots to a range of primates that swing through the branches in search of food. This upper level is a hotspot for pollination, as insects, bats, and birds contribute to the rainforest's regenerative cycle by transferring pollen among plants.

The forest understory, a darker, more humid environment, supports species adapted to lower light levels. Here, animals like jaguars, ocelots, and tapirs roam, while frogs, insects, and lizards find refuge in the damp foliage. This layer is also where many of the Amazon's medicinal plants grow. Indigenous communities have long known the value of these plants, using them in traditional medicine and ceremonies. Some of these species, like the cinchona tree (the source of quinine), have even influenced modern medicine, demonstrating the Amazon's vital role in global health.

On the forest floor, the ecosystem reaches its most intricate and subtle expressions. Fallen leaves and decaying plant matter create a nutrient-rich layer that supports fungi, insects, and decomposers, which recycle nutrients back into the soil. Leafcutter ants—remarkably organized insects that cultivate underground fungus gardens—play a critical role here, breaking down plant matter and aerating the soil. This base layer, though often overlooked, is essential to the Amazon's health, supporting a delicate cycle of decomposition and growth that sustains plant and animal life above.

22

Biodiversity in the Amazon is not only astounding in its scale but also in its interconnectedness. Each species, from the smallest insect to the largest predator, contributes to the balance of this ecosystem. For example, trees in the rainforest depend on animals like agoutis, rodents that hoard seeds, to disperse them across the forest floor. Likewise, large herbivores like tapirs and capybaras influence the distribution of plants through their grazing habits. Even predators like jaguars play a vital role in maintaining the health of prey populations, preventing any single species from dominating the landscape and ensuring biodiversity remains balanced.

This intricate web of life is especially evident in the Amazon's unique floodplain forests, or "varzea" forests. During the rainy season, these low-lying areas are flooded as the river rises, creating a seasonal habitat that fish and other aquatic species rely on for breeding and feeding. When the waters recede, these areas transform into rich feeding grounds for terrestrial animals, offering a bounty of fish and plant matter left behind by the flood. This annual cycle of flooding and retreat shapes the lives of countless species, driving the rhythms of survival and reproduction in the rainforest.

Human presence in the Amazon has also influenced its ecosystem, as indigenous communities have coexisted with the forest for thousands of years. Rather than deplete its resources, many Amazonian tribes have developed sustainable practices that enhance biodiversity. Traditional slash-and-burn agriculture, for example, when practiced on a small scale, has created patches of secondary forest that attract different species and increase habitat diversity. These communities possess an intimate knowledge of the forest's ecology, viewing themselves as part of a larger system in which every plant, animal, and natural process has a purpose.

The Amazon's biodiversity also holds immense potential for scientific research and medical discoveries. Thousands of plant species within the rainforest have medicinal properties, and many have yet to be studied thoroughly. This vast "natural pharmacy" could offer solutions to diseases and health challenges facing humanity. However, as the Amazon faces deforestation and climate change, much of its untapped knowledge risks being lost forever. Conservation efforts are increasingly focused on protecting not only the land but also the traditional knowledge of indigenous people, whose understanding of the ecosystem is invaluable.

Exploring the Amazon's ecosystem is like stepping into a living laboratory where nature's resilience and adaptability are on full display. This rich tapestry of life is sustained by delicate balances and ancient processes that highlight the beauty and fragility of the natural world. For visitors, witnessing the Amazon's biodiversity firsthand is a reminder of the importance of preserving it—not only for its intrinsic value but also for the survival of our planet's delicate ecological balance.

Best Time to Visit and Seasonal Considerations
Choosing the best time to visit the Amazon River depends on what you hope to experience, as the region has two distinct seasons: the high-water season (December to May) and the low-water season (June to November). Both seasons offer unique opportunities and challenges, and understanding the advantages and conditions of each can help you plan a more fulfilling, memorable, and safe Amazon adventure.

High-Water Season (December to May)
The high-water season, which is influenced by the Amazon Basin's rainy months, is widely regarded as the best time to explore the river and reach deeper into the rainforest. During these months, the river and its tributaries expand, flooding the surrounding forests and forming a vast network of waterways that allow boats to travel deeper into the jungle. If you want to see as much of the Amazon's interior as possible, this season is ideal.

Benefits of the High Water Season:
1. Increased Boat Accessibility: As water levels rise, creeks and smaller tributaries become navigable, allowing boats to reach more remote parts of the rainforest. These hidden areas are often teeming with wildlife and vegetation that are not normally accessible during the low-water season.

2. Exceptional Wildlife Viewing: Flooding drives fish and aquatic animals to the surface and closer to the banks, attracting predatory birds and mammals as well. This is an excellent time to observe caimans, capybaras, monkeys, and even jaguars hunting along the shoreline. This season is also ideal for birdwatching because migratory species are frequently present and vibrant flocks gather to feed.

3. Comfortable Temperatures and Fewer Mosquitoes: Although the high-water season brings rain, temperatures can be slightly cooler, often ranging from 75°F to 85°F (24°C to 29°C), making hiking and boating trips more enjoyable. Furthermore, while mosquitos are always present in the rainforest, the high-water season has fewer of them than the drier months, particularly in areas with good water circulation.

Considerations and precautions:

1. Increased Rain and Humidity: As expected, the high-water season brings frequent rain showers that can last for minutes to hours. Pack a lightweight raincoat, waterproof shoes, and quick-drying clothing. Be prepared for unexpected weather changes, as rain can fall without warning.

2. Some Trails May Be Inaccessible: Flooding has submerged many jungle trails, limiting opportunities for land-based activities such as hiking and camping. If trekking through the forest is important to you, consider the low-water season instead.

3. Bring Waterproof Gear: Electronics, documents, and other important items should be stored in waterproof cases. This advice is especially important for photographers, as humid and rainy weather can quickly damage sensitive equipment.

Low-Water Season (June-November)

The low-water season, which lasts from June to November, is distinguished by drier weather and lower river levels. As the water recedes, the Amazon reveals sandy beaches, previously hidden riverbanks, and trails that are once again open for exploration. This is the ideal season for those who want to combine river exploration with hiking, beach trips, and other land-based activities.

Advantages of the Low Water Season:

1. Ideal for Hiking and Land Excursions: As water levels fall, trails and pathways that were submerged during the high-water season are now visible. This is an ideal time for hiking through the rainforest, where guides can lead you to hidden waterfalls, unique plant life, and breathtaking viewpoints that showcase the jungle's vastness.

2. River Beaches and Swimming Opportunities: As the river recedes, sandy beaches form along its banks, providing areas for swimming, picnicking, and relaxation. During this season, many cruises include beach excursions, allowing guests to relax while taking in the breathtaking scenery.

3. Increased Wildlife Concentration at Watering Holes: Animals are frequently drawn to remaining water sources, making them easier to spot in specific areas. Mammals such as tapirs, capybaras, and monkeys are more likely to congregate around shrinking water holes, and predators like jaguars may become more visible as they hunt.

Considerations and precautions:

1. Higher Temperatures and Mosquito Activity: Drier weather brings warmer temperatures, which can reach 90°F (32°C) or higher. This is also the peak season for mosquitos, especially in areas with stagnant water. Bring insect repellent, long-sleeved shirts, and lightweight, breathable clothing to ensure your comfort and safety. If you're going camping or staying in a rustic lodge, consider using a mosquito net.

2. Limited River Access: During the low-water season, some smaller waterways become inaccessible, limiting boating opportunities. If you want to explore more remote areas of the forest or canoe through narrow channels, you might prefer the high-water season.

3. Hydration and Sun Protection: During the dry season, you'll need to stay hydrated because the heat can quickly cause dehydration during outdoor activities. Bring a reusable water bottle and fill it frequently. Sunscreen, a wide-brimmed hat, and sunglasses are also recommended to protect against the harsh Amazonian sunlight.

Additional tips for both seasons.

Choose Your Priorities: Each season provides unique experiences, so consider your interests. If you enjoy river excursions, hidden coves, and deep jungle access, the high-water season is ideal. If you prefer land-based activities, the low-water season provides more opportunities for hiking and beach excursions.

Consult with your tour operator: Amazon River cruises vary, and many operators provide different itineraries depending on the season. Some may include additional stops, excursions, or onboard activities based on seasonal conditions. Consulting with your operator can help ensure that your trip is tailored to your specific interests.

Respect the Local Ecosystem: The Amazon is a fragile and vital ecosystem, so be aware of your impact. To help the environment, stay on designated trails, avoid disturbing wildlife, and listen to your guides.

Ultimately, the Amazon River provides unforgettable experiences year-round, whether you're gliding through flooded forests, hiking ancient trails, or relaxing on pristine river beaches. With the proper planning and awareness of seasonal differences, your Amazon adventure can be both enriching and harmonious with this extraordinary ecosystem.

Essential Documents and Vaccinations

A well-prepared Amazon River cruise requires some essential documentation and careful attention to health precautions, as you'll be entering a unique and remote region with specific travel requirements. Proper documentation and vaccinations will help ensure your trip goes smoothly, so you can focus on enjoying the journey without unnecessary risks or complications. Here's a detailed guide on what to prepare and what to expect.

1. Travel Documents

Passport Requirements
A valid passport is required to enter the Amazon Basin countries, which include Brazil, Peru, and Colombia. Check your passport's expiration date; most countries require it to be valid for at least six months after your intended departure date. It is a good idea to keep both physical and digital copies of your passport in case it is lost or stolen.

Visa and Entry Permits
Visa requirements vary depending on your nationality and the country (or countries) to which your cruise will travel. Brazil, for example, requires a visa for travellers from certain countries, while others can enter without a visa. Similarly, Peru and Colombia have their own visa policies, so be sure to check the most recent requirements for each country on your itinerary. Many countries provide e-visas or visas on arrival, but it is best to confirm and apply for any required permits well in advance.

Vaccination Certificate Requirements:
Many Amazon countries, particularly Brazil and Peru, require travellers to show proof of yellow fever vaccination, especially if they are coming from a country where the disease is common. This proof is typically documented with a "yellow card" or an International Certificate of Vaccination. Without this, you may be denied entry, so get vaccinated at least ten days before your trip, as the vaccine takes time to take effect. Remember to keep this yellow card with your travel documents.

Copies of important documents
In addition to your passport, consider making copies of other important documents such as your travel insurance, vaccination records, and emergency contact information. Keep both digital and hard copies in a secure location, as remote areas in the Amazon frequently lack reliable internet access.

2. Health & Vaccinations

The Amazon Basin is home to a number of tropical diseases, so having up-to-date vaccinations and medications is critical for a safe and healthy experience. Consult a travel clinic or healthcare provider well before your departure to help you prepare.

Required vaccinations:

Yellow Fever: As previously stated, yellow fever vaccination is often required, particularly in Brazil and Peru. In most cases, the vaccine provides lifelong immunity, and the majority of travellers experience few side effects.

Recommended vaccines:

Hepatitis A and B are transmitted via contaminated food, water, or bodily fluids. Vaccines for these diseases are strongly advised, as access to medical care can be limited in the Amazon, making serious illnesses difficult to treat.

Typhoid fever is a bacterial infection that can be transmitted via contaminated food or water. Because access to clean water and hygiene facilities may differ depending on your cruise and activities, getting vaccinated is a wise precaution.

Tetanus is commonly contracted through cuts or wounds sustained on hikes or other activities in the Amazon. Tetanus vaccinations are frequently included in routine immunizations, so make sure yours is up to date.

Rabies: Although rabies is uncommon, it can be spread by wild animals, including bats, in remote areas. If you intend to participate in activities that may involve close encounters with wildlife, such as camping, your healthcare provider may recommend a rabies vaccination.

Malaria Precautions

Malaria is present in some areas of the Amazon, so talk to your doctor about preventive medications, especially if you'll be staying in more remote or mosquito-infested locations. Malaria prophylaxis can include a daily or weekly dose, depending on the medication. Follow your doctor's instructions carefully before and after your trip, as some malaria medications must be taken even after you leave the region.

Dengue Fever and Other Mosquito-borne Illnesses
Other mosquito-borne diseases that may exist in the Amazon include dengue fever, the Zika virus, and chikungunya. Unfortunately, there are no vaccines for these, so precautions are necessary. Pack a high-quality insect repellent with DEET or picaridin, wear long sleeves and pants, and consider treated clothing or mosquito nets, particularly in sleeping areas.

3. Additional health precautions

Altitude Sickness
If your trip to the Amazon begins in a high-altitude city such as Cusco, Peru, be aware of the possibility of altitude sickness. While this will not have a direct impact on your Amazon cruise, spending time at high elevations before descending into the rainforest can cause altitude-related symptoms. Allow yourself time to acclimatize before descending to lower altitudes, and stay hydrated.

Water and Food Safety
The Amazon is a tropical environment, so waterborne illnesses are a concern. Drink only bottled or purified water, including when brushing your teeth. Avoid raw foods and opt for well-cooked meals, particularly in rural or remote areas. If you plan to venture off the main cruise paths, bring a portable water filter or purification tablets.

Travel Insurance
Comprehensive travel insurance is strongly advised, especially in remote areas like the Amazon, where access to healthcare is limited. Make sure your policy includes medical expenses, medical evacuation, and trip interruption or cancellation. A medical evacuation may be required in the event of a serious illness or injury, as the Amazon lacks nearby major medical facilities and transportation can be difficult.

4. Final preparations and precautions.

Consult a Travel Clinic Early.
Ideally, go to a travel clinic at least 6-8 weeks before your trip. This allows for any required or recommended vaccinations, as well as the opportunity to discuss specific health concerns based on your medical history and itinerary.

Prepare a health kit.
Given the Amazon's remote location, carrying a health kit containing essentials such as pain relievers, anti-diarrheal medication, bandages, antiseptics, and rehydration salts is strongly advised. Include any prescription medications you need, with enough to last the entire trip, as refills may not be available.

Stay informed about current health risks.
Diseases and health risks change from year to year, so check for travel health advisories before leaving. Websites such as the CDC and WHO provide up-to-date information on health risks in the Amazon, ensuring that you have the most recent recommendations.

Travelling to the Amazon River is a rewarding and life-changing experience, and taking these precautions will ensure your safety. Proper documentation and health preparations are critical for peace of mind, allowing you to fully appreciate the natural wonders and cultural richness of this extraordinary region.

CHAPTER 2.

TIPS AND TRICKS TO EXPLORE AMAZON RIVER CRUISE

Fun Facts About the Amazon River Cruise

1. The Amazon River is so vast that it discharges more water than the next seven largest rivers combined.

2. The river spans over 4,000 miles, making it one of the longest rivers in the world, rivaling the Nile.

3. The Amazon Basin covers an area of roughly 2.7 million square miles, about the size of Australia.

4. Scientists estimate that one in ten known species on Earth lives in the Amazon rainforest.

5. Pink river dolphins, also known as "botos," are a unique species found only in the Amazon.

6. The Amazon River has no bridges crossing it, despite its enormous length and significance.

7. During the rainy season, the river can expand up to 25 miles in width in some areas.

8. The Amazon produces around 20% of the world's oxygen, earning it the nickname "the lungs of the Earth."

9. The river and its basin are home to over 3,000 fish species, with new ones discovered regularly.

10. The Amazon rainforest contains around 390 billion individual trees representing over 16,000 species.

11. Indigenous people of the Amazon have lived in the region for over 11,000 years.

12. The Amazon rainforest houses the largest concentration of tropical trees in the world.

13. The "Meeting of the Waters" near Manaus, Brazil, is where the dark Rio Negro and sandy Solimões River flow side by side without mixing.

14. The Amazon rainforest helps regulate rainfall across South America and even influences global weather patterns.

15. Some parts of the Amazon River reach depths of over 300 feet.

16. Piranhas, often feared, are actually an important part of the Amazon's ecosystem, helping to keep the river healthy.

17. The Amazon is home to the massive arapaima fish, which can grow up to 10 feet long.

18. The rainforest is so dense that in some places, only 1% of sunlight reaches the forest floor.

19. Many animals in the Amazon are adapted to swim, even though they're terrestrial, due to seasonal flooding.

20. The Amazon Basin is believed to have hidden cities and undiscovered civilizations beneath its dense canopy.

Getting Around Safely and Efficiently

Navigating the Amazon River safely and efficiently requires preparation and a good understanding of the unique environment. While the Amazon offers breathtaking sights and unforgettable experiences, it's essential to approach it with respect and care, especially if you're venturing far from populated areas. Here's a guide to help you make the most of your journey while prioritizing safety.

1. Choose a Reliable Tour Operator

The most secure and efficient way to explore the Amazon River is with a reputable tour operator or cruise company. These companies provide experienced guides, well-maintained boats, and necessary safety equipment, allowing travelers to focus on the experience. Look for operators with positive reviews and local knowledge, as they are better prepared to deal with the unique challenges of Amazon navigation, such as changing water levels and encountering local wildlife.

2. Follow the crew's instructions.

Amazon river guides and crew members are intimately familiar with the region and the potential hazards that come with it. Pay close attention to their instructions, particularly those involving safety protocols, wildlife interactions, and environmental precautions. Following their advice keeps you safe while minimizing your impact on this delicate ecosystem.

3. Use Proper Gear and Clothing.

The Amazon's climate is hot and humid, with frequent rainfall. Wearing lightweight, quick-drying clothing in light colors can help you stay comfortable while also protecting you from mosquitos and other insects. Wear long sleeves and pants to avoid bites, and always bring a wide-brimmed hat, sunglasses, and sunscreen for sun protection. Comfortable, waterproof shoes or sandals with a good grip are recommended, as the terrain can range from muddy forest paths to slippery boat decks.

4. Exercise caution with water and food.

To avoid water-borne illnesses, drink only bottled or purified water. Reputable tour companies will usually provide safe drinking water, but it's a good idea to bring a personal water filter or purification tablets on remote excursions. To reduce the risk of illness when eating local foods, particularly in villages, opt for well-cooked items and avoid raw vegetables or fruits that have not been peeled.

5. Keep valuables secure.

While the Amazon is relatively safe from theft, it is best to keep valuables secure, especially on multi-day cruises where you may dock in small towns or travel through remote areas. Use a waterproof bag for essentials such as passports, phones, and cameras, and keep your valuables in a secure pouch or backpack, particularly during boat transfers.

6. Prepare for mosquitoes and insects.

Mosquitoes in the Amazon can transmit diseases like malaria and dengue, so proper protection is required. Bring a strong insect repellent containing DEET or picaridin and apply it frequently, particularly in the early morning and evening hours when mosquitos are most active. If you're camping or staying in rustic accommodations, consider wearing insect repellent clothing or sleeping under a portable mosquito net.

7. Respect Wildlife Boundaries.

The Amazon is home to a diverse range of wildlife, some of which are dangerous if provoked. Keep a safe distance from animals, even if they appear calm, and never try to touch or feed them. Piranhas, caimans, and snakes are just a few of the species you might see, so follow your guide's advice on when and where it's safe to observe them closely. Be especially cautious during nighttime excursions, as many animals become more active after dark.

8. Plan for limited connectivity.
Many areas along the Amazon have unreliable cell service and internet, so plan accordingly. Before you leave, inform someone of your itinerary and expected return dates, and keep a list of emergency contacts in case of unforeseen circumstances. Bring extra power banks to charge your devices, as electricity may be limited on certain boats and in remote villages.

9. Pack essentials for emergencies
In addition to travel insurance, bring a basic first-aid kit that includes bandages, antiseptics, pain relievers, and any personal medications. In remote areas, medical assistance may be hours away, so being prepared can make a big difference if you sustain minor injuries or illnesses.

Following these guidelines will assist you in navigating the Amazon River safely and efficiently, allowing you to fully appreciate the wonders of this remarkable region while minimizing risks. Respect for local customs, wildlife, and the natural environment will enhance your experience and ensure a safe and memorable journey through the Amazon.

Staying Safe in a Unique Environment

Staying safe in the Amazon's unique and unpredictable environment requires a blend of awareness, respect, and preparation. With its dense rainforests, vast waterways, and exotic wildlife, the Amazon offers an extraordinary experience, but it's essential to keep safety a priority to fully enjoy your journey.

First, understand that the Amazon is not like other tourist destinations. Due to its remote location and distinct ecosystems, visitors should proceed with caution and humility. Hiring an experienced, reputable guide is invaluable because they are aware of the region's specific hazards, such as hidden wildlife and treacherous terrain. Your guide's local knowledge will help you navigate safely while learning about the area's amazing flora and fauna.

It is also critical to maintain vigilance towards wildlife. The Amazon is home to a diverse range of creatures, from colorful birds to elusive jaguars; however, many animals, such as snakes, spiders, and caimans, can be dangerous if disturbed. Always keep a safe distance from any animal and avoid making sudden movements or loud noises that may startle them. Never touch or feed wildlife, as this can result in unpredictable behavior and harm. Stick to your guide's suggested observation points for safe encounters with the Amazon's fascinating inhabitants.

Insect protection is another critical component of Amazon safety. Mosquitoes are common and can transmit diseases such as malaria and dengue fever, so use insect repellent regularly, especially at dawn and dusk when mosquitos are most active. To protect your skin, wear long-sleeved, lightweight, light-colored clothing. If you're camping or staying in a rustic setting, use mosquito nets at night for extra protection. Staying hydrated and avoiding strong scents (which attract insects) will also make your stay in the Amazon more enjoyable.

Weather in the Amazon can change quickly, so be prepared for unexpected rain showers and high humidity. Waterproof clothing, durable rain gear, and quick-dry clothing will help you stay comfortable and reduce the risk of illness from prolonged wet conditions. Heat exhaustion is also a concern, particularly during hikes or excursions under the canopy. Drink plenty of purified water, pace yourself, and take frequent breaks in shaded areas to avoid overheating.

Maintaining awareness of your surroundings is critical, especially when traveling through dense jungle trails or riverbanks. Slippery surfaces, uneven ground, and fallen branches are common, so wear strong, waterproof shoes with a good grip and avoid stepping blindly. Always follow your guide's instructions for where to walk and avoid deviating from established trails; this will reduce the likelihood of encountering venomous creatures or entering dangerous terrain.

When it comes to food and water safety, be mindful of what you consume. Drink only bottled or purified water, and avoid ice unless you are certain it was made with safe water. Local cuisine is a wonderful part of the Amazon experience, but when dining in remote villages or local markets, stick to cooked foods to reduce the risk of foodborne illness. Bring your own snacks for longer trips, as food options may be limited or unfamiliar in more remote areas.

While exploring, keep in mind that respect for the environment increases safety. The Amazon is a delicate ecosystem, and following Leave No Trace principles helps to protect its beauty and biodiversity. When interacting with indigenous communities, avoid littering, damaging plants or trees, and respect local customs. Simple practices such as taking your trash with you and not disturbing natural habitats help keep you and the ecosystem safe and protected.

Staying safe in the Amazon ultimately requires preparation, respect, and adaptability. To make the most of your Amazon adventure, approach it with an open mind, pay close attention to your guide, and exercise caution. With these practices, you'll be well-prepared to explore the Amazon's wonders in a responsible and enriching manner.

Interacting with Local Communities

Interacting with local communities along the Amazon River offers a rare opportunity to experience the culture, traditions, and knowledge of indigenous and riverine people who have lived harmoniously with the rainforest for generations. These communities are the true custodians of the Amazon, with a deep understanding of the environment that shapes their way of life. To ensure respectful, meaningful interactions, approach these encounters with an open heart, humility, and a willingness to learn. Here's how to do it with the utmost respect and sensitivity.

Native Tribal Man in Amazonia Rainforest in Handmade Boat

Begin by acknowledging that you are a visitor in these communities. Local customs, traditions, and social norms may differ significantly from what you're used to, so treat each interaction with respect and attention. Many indigenous communities welcome visitors as a chance to share their culture and stories, but they also value privacy and may prefer not to be the subject of constant photographs or inquiries. If you want to take a photo, always get permission first. Certain ceremonies or private spaces in some communities may be considered sacred and not open to photography; respect these boundaries to demonstrate your understanding of their importance.

Even if the majority of residents speak Spanish or Portuguese, learning a few basic words or phrases in the local language can greatly improve communication. A simple greeting, thank you, or respectful gesture can demonstrate your genuine interest in their culture and help to establish rapport. People appreciate it when visitors make an effort, no matter how small, to communicate in their language. Even better, some guides or local hosts may provide a quick lesson on phrases that will be particularly useful to the community.

Another important aspect of respectful interaction is adhering to traditional practices and being aware of local customs. Some communities, for example, have established rules regarding physical contact and personal space. When in doubt, follow your guide's or host's cues and observe their interactions. Basket weaving, cooking, and storytelling are examples of traditional practices that can be shared through community tourism activities. Engage wholeheartedly, listen attentively, and express gratitude for these demonstrations, which are frequently shared as a sign of trust and cultural pride.

Be mindful when giving gifts or offering support. Some travelers may feel compelled to donate money, clothing, or toys, particularly to children. However, these well-intentioned gestures can occasionally disrupt a community's balance or lead to reliance on outside aid. If you want to make a positive contribution, consult with your guide or community leaders first. Many ecotourism communities have established funds or support channels to direct resources to health, education, or community projects, ensuring that your contributions are both beneficial and culturally appropriate.

Purchasing locally made crafts, food, or other products is one of the most effective ways to directly support these communities. Handcrafted items such as jewelry, woven baskets, and pottery frequently reflect cultural artistry and skill passed down through the generations. Purchasing these items not only generates income, but also helps to preserve traditional crafts and cultural practices. When purchasing souvenirs, inquire about the significance of specific symbols or designs, which frequently have meaning unique to the community. These conversations enrich your travel experience by providing cultural insights.

Patience and flexibility are also required when visiting remote communities, as the pace of life here may be slower than you are used to. Respect their schedules, as daily activities such as fishing, farming, and ceremonial gatherings are prioritized. Sharing their time and space with visitors is a generous act for community members, who frequently disrupt their daily routines to accommodate them. Practicing patience and understanding demonstrates gratitude for their hospitality.

Finally, consider the environmental impact of your visit. Avoid leaving any waste behind, as disposal can be difficult in remote areas. Carry reusable water bottles, utensils, and bags to reduce single-use plastics and other environmentally harmful items. Respect the community's sustainable practices, such as composting or water conservation, which are often built into their way of life. Following these principles not only keeps the community clean, but it also demonstrates that you appreciate their stewardship of the Amazon.

By embracing these practices, you not only show respect for the Amazonian people, but you also gain a deeper, more authentic connection to the river and forest. Through respectful and thoughtful interactions, you'll gain a deeper appreciation for Amazon communities' unique culture, wisdom, and hospitality, making your journey truly unforgettable.

What Not To Do: Cultural and Safety-Based Tips

When visiting the Amazon River and its surrounding communities, understanding what not to do is just as important as knowing how to act respectfully and safely. The Amazon's unique culture and ecosystem require visitors to adapt their behavior to avoid disrupting local life, harming the environment, or putting themselves at risk. Here are key cultural and safety-based tips on what not to do, ensuring a respectful and safe Amazon experience.

Avoid Assuming Cultural Similarities
The Amazon Basin is home to hundreds of indigenous groups and riverine communities, each with their own customs, traditions, and beliefs. Avoid assuming that people here follow the same cultural norms as in your home country. For example, some communities may have different social rules regarding eye contact, personal space, and physical greetings. Respect these differences by observing first and then following your guide or host's lead.

Do not photograph people without permission.
Photography is an integral part of travel, but taking photos without permission can be intrusive and disrespectful. Some Amazonian communities refuse to be photographed for cultural or spiritual reasons. Always ask before photographing people, homes, or ceremonial spaces.

Respecting privacy is a simple but important way to demonstrate respect and foster trust.

Do not give money or gifts to children.
Giving money, candy, toys, or other gifts to children, while well-intentioned, can lead to dependency or foster a "begging culture." Direct gifts to children can also cause problems in family and community dynamics. If you feel compelled to help the community, speak with your guide or a local organization about how to do so in an effective and respectful manner, such as by purchasing locally made crafts or contributing to community funds.

Avoid loud and disruptive behavior.
Loud noises can disturb wildlife in the Amazon rainforest, disrupting the peaceful atmosphere that many local communities value. Avoid shouting, playing loud music, or using distracting devices. Many animals are sensitive to sound, so keeping noise levels low allows you to blend into the natural environment, increasing your chances of spotting wildlife while also respecting the tranquility valued by locals.

Don't touch or feed wildlife.
The Amazon is a delicate ecosystem, and handling or feeding wildlife can disrupt natural behaviors and pose health risks to both animals and humans. Feeding animals encourages them to approach people, which can lead to dangerous interactions. Similarly, touching animals or plants can be harmful because some species are venomous or carry diseases. Follow your guide's instructions closely and keep a safe distance.

Avoid picking plants and removing natural items.
It may be tempting to take a leaf, rock, or seed as a souvenir, but removing items from the Amazon can be detrimental to the environment. Plants, seeds, and even soil all contribute to the rainforest's health. Avoid picking plants, removing anything from the forest, or gathering "souvenirs" from nature. Instead, preserve your memories with environmentally friendly photos and stories.

Do not ignore the safety warnings about water and food.
Because of the Amazon's remote location, medical assistance may be difficult to obtain, so food and water safety should be prioritized. Avoid drinking untreated river water and instead opt for bottled or filtered water. Be cautious when handling raw foods or unfamiliar dishes, especially in remote areas where hygiene standards may vary. Ignoring these safety precautions could result in illness and a disrupted trip, so listen to your guide's advice on what is safe to consume.

The Amazon's tropical climate can make sunburn and insect bites worse. Avoid prolonged exposure to direct sunlight, and always wear sunscreen, hats, and lightweight, long-sleeved clothing. Additionally, use insect repellent to avoid mosquito, tick, and other insect bites. Ignoring these precautions increases your chances of getting sunburned, contracting mosquito-borne illnesses, and experiencing discomfort from bites.

Do not disregard environmental sustainability.
The Amazon is a fragile ecosystem, so avoid using single-use plastics and dispose of waste responsibly. Don't litter or leave trash, and if possible, bring reusable items such as water bottles and containers. Many communities have limited waste disposal options, so anything you bring should be left with you. Leaving no trace preserves the Amazon's beauty and biodiversity for future visitors.

Do not enter private or sacred spaces without an invitation.
Many Amazonian communities have designated areas for rituals and community gatherings, which can be private or sacred. Never enter spaces that appear closed off or that your guide has not invited you into. Respecting these boundaries demonstrates an understanding of local values and promotes positive relationships between visitors and communities.
Avoid wandering alone.
The Amazon is vast and full of unfamiliar terrain, so avoid wandering alone, even if the area appears safe. Jungle paths can be confusing, and it's easy to get disoriented. Certain areas may also contain hidden dangers, ranging from venomous creatures to fast-moving water. Stay close to your guide and other travelers, and follow the paths and areas they recommend.

Following these "What Not to Do" guidelines will help to ensure a respectful, safe, and responsible travel experience. Respecting local customs, wildlife, and environmental practices ensures that you have a positive impact while immersing yourself in the wonders of the Amazon River and its inhabitants.

CHAPTER 3.

CHOOSING THE RIGHT CRUISE: OPTIONS AND RECOMMENDATIONS

Overview of Amazon River Cruise Types

Choosing the right cruise for your Amazon adventure is an essential step in crafting an experience that matches your interests, comfort level, and expectations. From luxury cruises with gourmet dining and spas to intimate eco-tours that bring you closer to the heart of the jungle, each type of Amazon River cruise offers a unique way to explore one of the world's most captivating natural wonders. Here's a guide to help you navigate the options and find the cruise that best suits your Amazon journey.

1. Luxury Amazon River Cruises

Luxury cruises combine comfort and an immersive yet relaxed Amazon experience. These ships typically have large cabins, fine dining, air conditioning, and sometimes even additional amenities such as spas and pools. Luxury cruises are designed to provide high levels of comfort and personalized service while allowing you to explore the Amazon on informative but relaxing guided excursions.

A significant benefit of luxury cruises is the knowledgeable staff on board, which frequently includes bilingual naturalists, wildlife specialists, and experienced crew members who cater to guests' needs and answer questions about the ecosystem. These cruises also offer small-group excursions, making wildlife viewing and jungle hikes more enjoyable and accessible. This type of cruise is ideal for those who want to experience the Amazon in a more relaxed and structured setting.

Tip: If you want to experience the Amazon's breathtaking scenery and biodiversity without sacrificing comfort, a luxury cruise is an excellent option. However, be prepared to spend more money, as these cruises are on the more expensive end of the spectrum.

2. Expedition Cruises.

Expedition cruises are ideal for travelers seeking a balance of comfort and adventure. These cruises, which typically include moderately comfortable accommodations and guided excursions, are all about exploration. They offer an authentic, immersive experience that allows you to explore deeper into the rainforest through activities such as wildlife hikes, birdwatching, kayaking, and night safaris.

Expedition cruises frequently cover more diverse areas of the river and have flexible schedules that allow for seasonal wildlife sightings and local weather conditions. Although the boats lack some luxury features, they are outfitted with ample amenities such as comfortable cabins, dining rooms, and observation decks. Expedition cruises, led by expert guides, offer an opportunity to learn about the Amazon's unique ecosystem while maintaining a high level of safety and comfort.

Tip: If you want a hands-on, nature-focused experience but don't mind fewer frills, an expedition cruise is an excellent compromise. The experience is typically more rugged than a luxury cruise, so pack accordingly for outdoor activities and changing conditions.

3. Eco Cruises

Eco-cruises are an excellent choice for travelers looking to explore the Amazon in an environmentally and socially responsible manner. These cruises are designed to have the least environmental impact while also supporting conservation and community initiatives. Eco-cruise vessels are typically smaller, use sustainable practices such as solar power, water purification systems, and biodegradable products, and frequently collaborate with local communities on eco-friendly excursions.

Eco-cruises offer immersive jungle experiences, often led by local guides who have firsthand knowledge of the forest and its resources. Visits to community projects, conservation education talks, and nature walks can all help you understand the forest's delicate balance. Eco-cruises are often less luxurious, but they are extremely rewarding for travelers who care about sustainability and environmental protection.

An eco-cruise is ideal if you care about the environment and want to support responsible tourism. Prepare for simpler accommodations, as these cruises prioritize eco-friendliness over luxury. Your experience will be rich in cultural and natural insights, making it an impactful way to explore the Amazon.

4. Boutique and Adventure Cruises.

Boutique and adventure cruises offer a more intimate, personalized experience, often on smaller boats carrying fewer passengers. These cruises are intended for travelers looking for an immersive, close-up adventure in the Amazon. With a limited number of guests, you can expect specialized itineraries, flexible schedules, and exclusive excursions tailored to the group's preferences.

Adventure cruises are heavily focused on exploration, with options for canoeing through narrow waterways, hiking remote jungle trails, and even camping in the rainforest. Boutique cruises are charming and unique, with locally inspired decor and meals that provide a more personalized experience of Amazonian life. Accommodations are often more rustic than on luxury cruises, but they provide a cozy, authentic atmosphere.

Tip: This type of cruise is ideal for adventurous travelers who value personalization and are open to a more rustic experience. If you enjoy exploring hidden channels or sleeping under the stars, a boutique or adventure cruise may be for you.

5. Budget-Friendly River Cruises

For budget-conscious travelers, there are affordable options that still provide an enjoyable Amazon experience. Budget cruises may lack the high-end amenities found on luxury vessels, but they still provide the essentials such as comfortable cabins, guided excursions, and scenic views. These cruises focus on the essentials, allowing you to explore the Amazon without exceeding your budget.

Budget cruises frequently use larger boats with more passengers, which can impact the level of personalization and intimacy of excursions. However, they still offer an excellent introduction to the Amazon, with activities such as nature hikes, village visits, and wildlife viewing. These cruises usually have shorter itineraries but still include key highlights along the river.

Tip: If you're flexible and want to experience the Amazon without all the extras, a low-cost cruise can be an excellent option. However, expect a less intimate experience, with larger group sizes and fewer amenities.

Final Advice for Choosing Your Cruise

When deciding on the best type of cruise for you, think about your priorities, such as comfort, adventure, environmental responsibility, and budget. Each cruise type provides a unique way to experience the Amazon, ranging from luxurious relaxation to close-up jungle adventures. Whatever your preference, a well-chosen cruise will ensure that you get the most out of your Amazon adventure, immersing you in the wonders of the rainforest in a way that suits your travel style.

Luxury vs. Budget-Friendly Options on the Amazon River

When choosing between luxury and budget-friendly options for an Amazon River cruise, the decision often boils down to the type of experience you want and how you prioritize comfort, amenities, and adventure. Each option provides a unique way to engage with the Amazon's beauty and culture, but understanding the differences will help you select a cruise that aligns with your expectations and travel goals.

Luxury Cruises: Immersive Comfort in the Heart of the Amazon

Luxury cruises on the Amazon offer a comfortable, personalized experience with high-end amenities. If you want to explore the Amazon's wonders without giving up any of the comforts you enjoy at home, a luxury cruise is the best option. These vessels are typically outfitted with spacious cabins that often have floor-to-ceiling windows or private balconies, allowing you to enjoy breathtaking views of the rainforest from the comfort of your own room.

The dining experience on a luxury cruise is also enhanced, with professionally trained chefs preparing gourmet meals that highlight local ingredients and Amazonian flavor. Many luxury cruises even provide personalized dining options, allowing guests to enjoy meals tailored to their dietary preferences, such as vegetarian, vegan, and gluten-free options. Aside from the food, amenities such as air conditioning, hot showers, spa services, and even pools on some vessels provide a level of comfort that allows you to fully relax and unwind after a day of exploration.

Luxury cruises are typically smaller, with fewer passengers, resulting in a more intimate experience. This also enables personalized service and attentive crew members who can meet your needs, ranging from special requests in your cabin to planned activities. Guided excursions are led by expert naturalists who are extremely knowledgeable about the Amazon's ecosystems, wildlife, and culture, resulting in a rich, educational experience with small group sizes for a more private, interactive feel.

Luxury cruises provide peace of mind to those who value convenience, safety, and high-quality service. These vessels are outfitted with advanced navigation and safety features, and their itineraries frequently include exclusive, remote areas of the Amazon that larger, more affordable boats cannot reach. Luxury cruises are ideal for travelers who want to immerse themselves in the Amazon without sacrificing comfort, ensuring that each moment is a luxurious experience surrounded by the magic of the rainforest.

Budget-Friendly Cruises: An affordable adventure with an authentic twist.

Budget-friendly cruises are an excellent way for travelers who value adventure and discovery over amenities to explore the Amazon on a low-budget basis. Budget cruises may lack luxury amenities, but they still provide a rewarding experience by focusing on the essentials: comfortable accommodations, knowledgeable guides, and enriching excursions that bring you closer to the Amazon's wildlife and culture.

Cabins on budget cruises are typically simple but comfortable, with beds, fans, and shared or private bathrooms. These vessels may lack air conditioning and hot showers, and cabins are typically smaller, but the rustic setting adds a sense of adventure that many travelers find appealing. While the dining is less gourmet than on luxury cruises, budget cruises still serve authentic Amazonian meals that highlight local flavors, such as fresh fish, fruits, and hearty stews, giving guests a taste of the region's cuisine.

A budget cruise often provides a more communal experience, with larger groups on board and shared dining and excursion times. This can be a fun way to meet other travelers, share stories, and bond over your mutual interest in exploring the Amazon. Excursions are less exclusive than luxury cruises, but they are still led by knowledgeable guides who will introduce you to the river's most captivating sights, such as birdwatching, guided nature walks, and village visits.

Budget-friendly cruises frequently use larger boats that can accommodate more passengers. This means the itinerary may be less flexible, covering popular spots rather than remote sections of the river. However, these cruises still offer numerous opportunities to experience the Amazon's breathtaking biodiversity. You might find yourself kayaking along riverbanks, fishing for piranhas, or navigating jungle trails with a local guide, all while admiring the raw beauty of the rainforest.

Budget cruises, while cost-effective, necessitate greater adaptability. You'll most likely have limited access to Wi-Fi, electricity, and other modern conveniences, so pack smartly and expect a more rustic experience. For the adventurous traveler who prefers a more grounded experience and is willing to forego high-end amenities, a low-cost cruise can be extremely rewarding, connecting you to the Amazon in a raw, authentic manner.

Final Thoughts: Which Option Is Right for You?
Choosing between luxury and budget-friendly options comes down to what you value most about your Amazon experience. A luxury cruise will provide you with relaxation, privacy, and attentive service in an environment that enhances the natural beauty of the Amazon, from refined comfort to carefully curated excursions.

On the other hand, if you want an authentic, back-to-basics adventure that gets you close to the Amazon's raw elements and allows you to explore on a tighter budget, a budget-friendly cruise provides a genuine, down-to-earth experience without the frills. It's the best option for travelers who are adaptable, enjoy meeting other adventurers, and are willing to embrace the Amazon's rugged charm.

Finally, both options offer unforgettable experiences with the Amazon's natural beauty, biodiversity, and culture. Whether you prefer the luxury of indulgence or the simplicity of adventure, the Amazon River has a cruise to suit your needs, providing you with unforgettable memories along one of the world's most extraordinary rivers.

Eco-Cruises and Sustainable Choices

Eco-cruises on the Amazon offer a unique opportunity to experience the rainforest in a way that minimizes environmental impact and promotes sustainable tourism. For travelers who value responsible travel, these cruises provide an immersive way to explore the Amazon while supporting conservation efforts and local communities. Designed with sustainability at their core, eco-cruises prioritize practices that protect the delicate Amazon ecosystem and honor the cultural heritage of its people. Here's what to expect from an eco-cruise and how to make the most of this environmentally conscious experience.

What Sets Eco-Cruises Apart?
Eco-cruises differ from traditional cruises in that they are specifically designed to reduce the environmental impact of your trip. Many eco-cruise companies use renewable energy sources, such as solar panels and energy-efficient systems, to reduce their reliance on fossil fuels. These vessels are frequently smaller, carrying fewer passengers, which reduces environmental impact and makes it easier to explore less accessible parts of the river without disturbing local habitats.

Onboard eco-cruises, sustainable practices extend to waste management, with the majority operating zero-waste policies that avoid plastic, incorporate recycling, and manage waste responsibly. Eco-cruises also prioritize water conservation, frequently employing advanced filtration systems to purify and reuse water, thereby reducing the strain on the river and its surrounding ecosystem. These practices enable visitors to experience the Amazon with a smaller footprint, knowing that their presence has little impact on the environment.

A Focus on Responsible Wildlife Viewing.
Eco-cruises place a strong emphasis on responsible wildlife viewing practices. Eco-cruise guides are trained to follow ethical wildlife observation guidelines, allowing guests to observe animals from a safe distance without disturbing their natural behavior. These cruises are designed to provide meaningful, low-impact interactions with the Amazon's flora and fauna, and they frequently include smaller, quieter excursions such as kayaking or canoeing that allow you to appreciate the rainforest without disturbing its inhabitants.

This approach benefits wildlife while also providing a more rewarding travel experience. Observing animals in their natural behavior, free of fear or interference from human activity, allows you to see the Amazon for what it is: a thriving, interconnected ecosystem. Eco-cruises prioritize environmental stewardship, educating guests on the importance of sustainable wildlife viewing and how small changes can have a big impact.

Supporting Local Communities
Eco-cruises typically work closely with indigenous and local communities to support sustainable tourism initiatives that benefit the local economy and culture. Many eco-cruises include visits to villages or community-led projects, which allow travelers to learn about Amazonian culture and the traditional knowledge of the people who live there. This fosters a connection between guests and locals while directly benefiting these communities.

When you book an eco-cruise, a portion of the proceeds are often directed toward local development projects such as health care, education, or conservation initiatives that protect the Amazon's natural resources. By taking an eco-cruise, you are supporting a tourism model that values and empowers Amazonian communities rather than exploiting them.

Educational Experiences and Conservation Awareness
Eco-cruises prioritize education, with on-board experts and guides providing insights into the Amazon's unique biodiversity, conservation

challenges, and sustainable practices. Eco-cruise passengers learn about the complex interplay of species in the rainforest through educational talks, guided hikes, and hands-on activities, as well as the importance of protecting native flora and indigenous communities' contributions to conservation.

This educational focus makes eco-cruises especially appealing to travelers seeking a deeper understanding of the Amazon beyond its scenic beauty. Eco-cruises empower guests to become advocates for the rainforest long after they leave by raising awareness about environmental issues such as deforestation, habitat loss, and the Amazon's role in global climate regulation.

Tips for Selecting the Right Eco-Cruise

When selecting an eco-cruise, look into the operator's sustainability credentials and specific practices. Look for companies that have been certified by reputable organizations like the Rainforest Alliance or the Global Sustainable Tourism Council, as these certifications indicate a commitment to high environmental and social standards. Reputable eco-cruise companies should have open policies regarding waste management, energy use, and community partnerships.

Inquire about how the cruise interacts with wildlife and whether they have any policies prohibiting feeding or handling animals. A genuine eco-cruise operator will put animal welfare first, ensuring that excursions do not disrupt the Amazon's delicate balance. In addition, inquire about the group's size; smaller groups are typically less disruptive to both the environment and local communities, allowing for a more intimate, meaningful experience.

Pack carefully and respect eco-practices.

Eco-cruise passengers should pack with sustainability in mind. Bring a reusable water bottle, avoid single-use plastics, and choose biodegradable or reef-safe toiletries, as water on eco-cruises is frequently returned to the river. It is also recommended that you wear lightweight, quick-dry clothing that protects you from insects and the sun.

Respect the eco-cruise's sustainability by adhering to waste, energy, and water usage guidelines. Many eco-cruises encourage guests to follow Leave No Trace principles, such as disposing of personal waste and not causing harm to plants or wildlife. These simple habits contribute to the cruise's mission of preserving the Amazon's natural beauty.

Final Thoughts about Eco-Cruises and Sustainable Choices
An Amazon eco-cruise is more than just a scenic journey; it represents a commitment to responsible travel and conservation. Eco-cruises are the ideal way for travelers to experience the Amazon's natural beauty and rich culture while also making a positive impact. By supporting these sustainable choices, you help to preserve the Amazon's delicate ecosystems and the unique heritage of its communities, ensuring that future generations can enjoy the Amazon's wonders just as we do today.

Recommended Cruise Operators

When planning an Amazon River cruise, selecting a reputable operator is crucial to ensure a safe, enriching, and memorable experience. Below is a curated list of distinguished cruise operators, each offering unique itineraries and amenities to cater to various preferences and budgets.

1. Aqua Expeditions
Aqua Expeditions is known for its luxury river cruises, which offer an intimate experience with a focus on personalized service. Their ships, including the Aria Amazon, offer spacious suites with panoramic views, gourmet dining curated by top chefs, and guided excursions led by expert naturalists. The company prioritizes sustainable tourism practices, ensuring minimal environmental impact while providing luxurious comfort.

2. Delfin Amazon Cruises.
Delfin's boutique vessels, which include the Delfin I, II, and III, combine luxury and adventure. Guests can expect elegantly designed cabins, fine dining experiences, and a variety of excursions, including kayaking, wildlife spotting, and visits to local communities. Delfin is committed to responsible tourism, collaborating closely with indigenous communities and prioritizing conservation efforts.

3. Rainforest Cruises

Rainforest Cruises specializes in authentic Amazon experiences and offers a range of vessels, from traditional riverboats to modern luxury ships. They offer customizable itineraries throughout Peru, Brazil, Ecuador, and Bolivia, catering to a variety of interests and budgets. Their cruises emphasize wildlife observation, cultural interactions, and environmentally friendly practices.

4. Adventure Life

Adventure Life provides expedition-style cruises that focus on immersive experiences in the Amazon. Their itineraries last 4 to 8 days and include visits to remote tributaries and national reserves. With a fleet that includes the luxurious Zafiro and the intimate La Perla, they cater to a wide range of comfort levels while remaining committed to sustainable tourism and community engagement.

5. G Adventures

G Adventures offers small-group expeditions that focus on cultural immersion and responsible travel. Their Amazon River cruises frequently include activities such as guided jungle walks, canoe excursions, and visits to indigenous villages. G Adventures is well-known for its commitment to sustainability and ethical tourism practices, which ensure that their trips benefit local communities and ecosystems.

6. Amazon Nature Tours.

Amazon Nature Tours operates the Motor Yacht Tucano and offers expedition cruises deep into the Brazilian Amazon. Their itineraries emphasize wildlife observation, birdwatching, and exploring lesser-known tributaries. The Tucano is designed for small groups, offering a cozy atmosphere with comfortable accommodations and knowledgeable guides.

7. Lindblade Expeditions

Lindblad Expeditions partners with National Geographic to offer voyages that combine luxury and education. Their Amazon itineraries include expert-led excursions, photography workshops, and opportunities to collaborate with local researchers. The ships are outfitted with modern amenities, ensuring a pleasant voyage through the rainforest.

8. Aqua Expeditions

Aqua Expeditions is known for its luxury river cruises, which offer an intimate experience with a focus on personalized service. Their ships, including the Aria Amazon, offer spacious suites with panoramic views, gourmet dining curated by top chefs, and guided excursions led by expert naturalists. The company prioritizes sustainable tourism practices, ensuring minimal environmental impact while providing luxurious comfort.

9. Delfin Amazon Cruises.

Delfin's boutique vessels, which include the Delfin I, II, and III, combine luxury and adventure. Guests can expect elegantly designed cabins, fine dining experiences, and a variety of excursions, including kayaking, wildlife spotting, and visits to local communities. Delfin is committed to responsible tourism, collaborating closely with indigenous communities and prioritizing conservation efforts.

10. Rainforest Cruises

Rainforest Cruises specializes in authentic Amazon experiences and offers a range of vessels, from traditional riverboats to modern luxury ships. They offer customizable itineraries throughout Peru, Brazil, Ecuador, and Bolivia, catering to a variety of interests and budgets. Their cruises emphasize wildlife observation, cultural interactions, and environmentally friendly practices.

11. Adventure Life

Adventure Life provides expedition-style cruises that focus on immersive experiences in the Amazon. Their itineraries last 4 to 8 days and include visits to remote tributaries and national reserves. With a fleet that includes the luxurious Zafiro and the intimate La Perla, they cater to a wide range of comfort levels while remaining committed to sustainable tourism and community engagement.

12. G Adventures

G Adventures offers small-group expeditions that focus on cultural immersion and responsible travel. Their Amazon River cruises frequently include activities such as guided jungle walks, canoe excursions, and visits to indigenous villages. G Adventures is well-known for its commitment to sustainability and ethical tourism practices, which ensure that their trips benefit local communities and ecosystems.

13. Amazon Nature Tours.

Amazon Nature Tours operates the Motor Yacht Tucano and offers expedition cruises deep into the Brazilian Amazon. Their itineraries emphasize wildlife observation, birdwatching, and exploring lesser-known tributaries. The Tucano is designed for small groups, offering a cozy atmosphere with comfortable accommodations and knowledgeable guides.

14. Lindblade Expeditions

Lindblad Expeditions partners with National Geographic to offer voyages that combine luxury and education. Their Amazon itineraries include expert-led excursions, photography workshops, and opportunities to collaborate with local researchers. The ships are outfitted with modern amenities, ensuring a pleasant voyage through the rainforest.

Considerations When Selecting a Cruise Operator

Itinerary and Duration: Select an operator whose itinerary matches your preferences and time constraints. Some cruises take short, scenic routes, while others delve deeper into remote areas of the Amazon, providing a more immersive experience. Consider whether you want a brief exploration or a longer journey, as cruise lengths range from a few days to more than a week.

Type of Experience: Each operator specializes in a specific type of experience, such as luxury, adventure, eco-tourism, and cultural immersion. Luxury operators like Aqua Expeditions and Delfin Cruises prioritize comfort and high-end amenities, whereas G Adventures and Amazon Nature Tours cater to travelers looking for hands-on, adventurous experiences. When choosing an operator, think about what type of environment and activities are most important to you.

Group Size and Vessel Type: Smaller vessels offer a more intimate, personalized experience and are usually quieter, allowing for better wildlife observation. Operators such as Lindblad Expeditions and Aqua Expeditions provide smaller vessels with fewer passengers, resulting in a more exclusive experience. Larger vessels can accommodate more passengers, which may reduce the intimacy of excursions but may be more cost-effective.

Sustainability Practices: If you value responsible tourism, look into eco-friendly operators such as Rainforest Cruises or Delfin Amazon Cruises, which use sustainable practices and support local communities. Eco-cruise operators frequently collaborate with conservation projects or directly invest in community development, ensuring that your trip benefits the region.

Knowledgeable guides are essential for an enriching Amazon experience because they improve wildlife spotting, cultural learning, and safety. Lindblad Expeditions, for example, works with National Geographic to ensure that their guides are experts in their fields, often with backgrounds in biology, anthropology, or environmental sciences. Inquire about the guides' background and training, as this can significantly impact your overall experience.

Onboard Amenities and Comfort: If creature comforts are a must, look for operators that provide air conditioning, gourmet dining, and spacious cabins. Luxury cruises, such as those offered by Aqua Expeditions and Delfin, provide first-rate amenities that allow you to completely relax while exploring the Amazon's wonders. Budget-friendly or adventure-focused operators may provide simpler accommodations, which are ideal for travelers who prefer an immersive, rugged experience over luxury.

Safety Standards: Reliable cruise operators prioritize safety, which includes well-maintained vessels, certified guides, and adequate safety equipment. Established operators with years of experience, such as Adventure Life or Amazon Nature Tours, typically have strict safety protocols, so it's a good idea to ask about them before booking.

By carefully evaluating these factors and researching operators with established reputations, you will be better able to select a cruise that meets your expectations, budget, and values. The right operator will ensure that your Amazon River adventure is not only memorable, but also safe, comfortable, and respectful of the incredible environment you're exploring.

Amenities, Onboard Experience, and Inclusions

The amenities and onboard experience on an Amazon River cruise can vary significantly depending on the type of cruise you select—whether it's a luxury, expedition, or eco-focused option. Understanding what's typically included in each type of cruise will help you make an informed decision and ensure that your journey is as enjoyable and comfortable as possible. Here's a breakdown of what to expect, along with some tips on how to maximize your onboard experience.

Cabins and Accommodation

On a luxury cruise, cabins are frequently spacious suites with panoramic windows or private balconies, allowing you to enjoy uninterrupted views of the Amazon's lush scenery right from your room. These cabins may also include premium linens, climate control, private bathrooms with hot showers, and, on certain vessels, private butler service. Luxury operators such as Aqua Expeditions and Delfin Cruises are well-known for their beautifully designed cabins, which offer a retreat-like experience in the heart of the jungle.

Expedition and eco-cruise cabins are generally simpler, with a focus on functionality rather than luxury. Cabins on these cruises are comfortable, but they may lack high-end amenities like air conditioning or large windows. For travelers who are more interested in the Amazon's immersive, adventure aspect, these cabins provide a cozy, functional space to rest without the added frills. They are usually equipped with fans, necessary furnishings, and clean private or shared bathrooms, depending on the vessel.

Dining Experience

Gourmet dining is a highlight of luxury Amazon cruises. Many luxury operators collaborate with renowned chefs to create menus inspired by Amazonian flavors, which include fresh, local ingredients such as fish, tropical fruits, and exotic herbs. Meals are frequently served in elegant dining rooms with attentive staff, and dietary restrictions are usually accommodated without difficulty. Guests can expect a diverse range of cuisines, including fusion dishes that combine Amazonian ingredients with international culinary techniques.

Dining on expedition and eco-cruises is usually simpler, but there is still a satisfying selection of Amazon-inspired dishes. Meals are usually communal, creating a social atmosphere among travelers. Food can be prepared using local ingredients, providing guests with authentic Amazonian flavors. While it may lack the refined presentation of a luxury cruise, the dining experience on these ships is hearty, wholesome, and frequently culturally insightful. Keep in mind that on budget-friendly or eco-friendly cruises, options may be limited, so communicate any dietary requirements to the operator in advance.

Onboard Amenities

Luxury cruises provide a variety of amenities to help you relax and unwind, even while navigating the Amazon. Depending on the vessel, amenities may include spa services, plunge pools, open-air lounges, and even gyms. These cruises typically include observation decks, which allow guests to relax while enjoying 360-degree views of the rainforest. Some luxury cruise lines may also offer optional activities such as yoga sessions, wellness treatments, and cocktail hours, providing a peaceful respite after a day of excursions.

Expedition cruises, while generally more modest, still provide necessary amenities for a comfortable journey. Most have observation decks or lounge areas where visitors can unwind, socialize, and take in the scenery. While they may not have luxury amenities such as spas or pools, these ships frequently offer educational talks, documentaries, and slide shows to enhance the onboard experience. Guests will also find standard amenities such as a small bar, a library with nature books, and indoor lounges.

Eco-cruises prioritize sustainability over lavish amenities. These vessels are typically smaller and have fewer amenities, but they are built with environmentally friendly materials and energy-efficient systems. On board, you may find solar-powered lights, compost toilets, and other environmentally friendly products. While these cruises may lack some creature comforts, they offer an excellent opportunity to explore the Amazon while minimizing environmental impact.

Excursion and Guided Activities

Most Amazon River cruises include daily guided excursions and activities as part of the cruise package, though the nature and intensity of these experiences vary. Luxury and expedition cruises frequently include a variety of activities such as wildlife viewing, canoeing, night safaris, and village excursions. Professional naturalists typically lead excursions and provide information about the Amazon's ecology, wildlife, and indigenous cultures. Having experienced guides is essential for safety and improves your understanding of the complex ecosystem you're exploring.

Eco-cruises typically prioritize activities with low environmental impact, such as kayaking, nature walks, and visits to conservation projects. These excursions are frequently led by local guides who share their indigenous knowledge of the rainforest. Keep in mind that while some budget or eco-focused cruises may have simpler activities and larger group sizes, the immersive nature of these tours is extremely rewarding for those looking for a grounded Amazon experience.

Inclusions and Optional Add-ons

The level of inclusions in an Amazon River cruise package varies by cruise type and operator. Luxury cruises typically offer all-inclusive packages that include meals, beverages, excursions, and, in some cases, gratuities. Other services, such as private transfers and specialty drinks, may be included. This all-inclusive approach makes planning easier and allows guests to relax without worrying about additional costs.

Expedition cruises typically include the basics, such as meals and guided activities, but may charge additional fees for alcoholic beverages, gratuities, or specialized excursions. Before booking, make sure to double-check what's included, as add-on fees can vary greatly.

Eco-cruises typically include meals and excursions, though some may have fewer overall inclusions. Due to their emphasis on sustainability, you may be charged additional fees for conservation contributions or community project donations. It's a good idea to inquire about any additional costs ahead of time so that you can plan accordingly.

Preparing for the Onboarding Experience

No matter which cruise type you choose, pack with care for the Amazon environment. Lightweight, quick-drying clothing, insect repellent, and a reusable water bottle are required, and for eco-cruises, biodegradable toiletries and minimal plastic are suggested. Embrace the adventure with an open mind—whether you're in a luxury suite with panoramic views or a simple cabin that brings you closer to nature, the Amazon provides a once-in-a-lifetime experience that goes beyond amenities.

CHAPTER 4

PACKING GUIDE FOR THE AMAZON RIVER ADVENTURE

Essentials for Comfort and Safety

Packing for an Amazon River adventure requires careful planning to ensure comfort and safety in a tropical rainforest environment. The Amazon's hot, humid climate, coupled with its dense vegetation and diverse wildlife, means that each item you bring can significantly impact your experience. Here's a guide to the essentials you'll need to make your journey through the Amazon both enjoyable and secure.

Lightweight, Quick-Dry Clothing

The Amazon's tropical climate is warm and humid throughout the year, with frequent rain showers. To stay comfortable, pack lightweight, moisture-wicking clothing that dries quickly. Long-sleeved shirts and pants are essential for protecting against the sun, insects, and possible scratches from dense foliage. Look for neutral, light-colored clothing that is less likely to attract insects and will keep you cool under the hot sun.

Waterproof Rain Gear

Rain is an essential component of the Amazon ecosystem, and even during the dry season, showers can occur unexpectedly. A lightweight, breathable rain jacket is essential for staying dry on excursions. Choose a jacket that can be packed compactly in your day bag, as rain can come and go unexpectedly. Some travelers bring a small, packable poncho, which can be useful during heavy rains and also serves as a backpack cover.

Comfortable, waterproof footwear

The terrain in the Amazon ranges from muddy trails to riverbanks and boat decks, so durable, waterproof footwear is essential. Closed-toe hiking shoes or boots with good traction will keep your feet safe and provide support on nature hikes. Also, bring a pair of quick-drying sandals with a good grip for boat activities or shorter excursions. Avoid flip-flops, as they provide insufficient support or protection in this environment.

Insect repellent containing DEET or picaridin

Mosquitoes and other insects are abundant in the Amazon, and some can transmit diseases such as malaria and dengue fever. To reduce bites, use a strong insect repellent containing DEET or picaridin. Apply liberally to exposed skin and clothing before engaging in any activity, particularly in the early morning and evening when mosquitos are most active. For added protection, consider treating your clothing with permethrin, an insect repellent that can significantly reduce bites.

Sun Protection Essentials

The Amazon's proximity to the equator results in intense sun exposure, even beneath the forest canopy. Pack a high-SPF, water-resistant sunscreen and apply liberally all day. A wide-brimmed hat is also recommended to protect your face and neck, as well as polarized sunglasses to protect your eyes from the sun's reflection on the water. Choose UV-protective sunglasses and consider using a strap to keep them secure during boat rides or hiking.

Reusable Water Bottle with Filter.

Staying hydrated is critical in the Amazon's humid climate, where dehydration can occur quickly. Bring a reusable water bottle with a built-in filter so you always have access to safe drinking water. Many environmentally conscious travelers prefer bottles with high-quality filtration systems, which allow them to refill directly from taps or streams as needed. Alternatively, pack water purification tablets for added safety in remote areas where bottled water may be unavailable.

First Aid Kit

A well-stocked first aid kit is essential for dealing with minor injuries or discomforts in a remote setting. Include essentials such as adhesive bandages, antiseptic wipes, gauze, and adhesive tape for cuts and scrapes. Pack pain relievers, anti-diarrheal medication, antihistamines, and any personal medications you may require. Rehydration salts are highly recommended because they help replenish electrolytes after dehydration or heat exhaustion.

Biodegradable toiletries

To reduce your environmental impact, bring biodegradable toiletries such as soap, shampoo, and toothpaste. These environmentally friendly products are less harmful to the delicate Amazon ecosystem if any residue ends up in natural water sources. Some eco-cruises require guests to use biodegradable products, so be prepared with eco-friendly alternatives.

Portable chargers or power banks

Power outlets may be limited on some vessels, particularly eco-cruises and smaller boats. A fully charged power bank allows you to keep essential electronics like your phone, camera, and GPS running. Choose a portable charger with multiple charges, as reliable power may not be available in all areas. Solar-powered chargers are also an option for longer-term adventures.

Headlamp or Flashlight with Extra Batteries

Nighttime in the Amazon can be extremely dark, so reliable lighting is essential for navigating the boat or going on an evening wildlife excursion. A headlamp is especially useful for keeping your hands free. Choose a water-resistant model with adjustable brightness, and bring extra batteries to ensure consistent lighting throughout your trip.

Dry bags and waterproof cases.

With the Amazon's frequent rain showers and the possibility of water-based excursions, dry bags and waterproof cases are essential for protecting your belongings. Use a dry bag to keep your phone, wallet, camera, and travel documents. Waterproof cases or ziplock bags are also useful for storing smaller items like maps, batteries, and snacks. Multiple sizes are useful because they allow you to organize items according to your daily activities.

Multipurpose scarf or bandana

A versatile scarf or bandana can be used for a variety of purposes on Amazon. Use it to protect your neck from the sun, keep sweat out of your eyes, cover your face for added dust or bug protection, or as a light cover-up. Quick-drying fabrics are ideal, and darker colors tend to stay cleaner for longer.

Packing these essentials ensures you're ready for the Amazon's unique challenges while remaining comfortable and safe. These items may appear simple, but they can significantly improve your experience, allowing you to enjoy Amazon's beauty without undue discomfort or risk.

Clothing and Gear for the Rainforest Climate

Packing the right clothing and gear is essential for a comfortable and enjoyable experience in the Amazon's hot, humid, and often rainy climate. The key is to choose items that are lightweight, moisture-wicking, quick-drying, and versatile, allowing you to adapt easily to the rainforest's shifting conditions. Here's a guide to the best clothing and gear to bring along for your Amazon adventure.

Lightweight, Breathable Layers
The Amazon's tropical climate is consistently warm and humid, so breathable, lightweight clothing is essential for staying comfortable. Choose moisture-wicking fabrics, such as polyester or merino wool, which draw sweat away from your skin and dry quickly. Avoid cotton because it retains moisture, making you feel damp and uncomfortable in humid weather. Instead, bring lightweight, long-sleeved shirts and pants to keep your skin safe from insects, sun exposure, and scratches from dense foliage.

Quick-drying shirts and pants
For daily excursions, opt for quick-dry, long-sleeved shirts and convertible pants. Long sleeves protect against the sun and insects, and many travelers prefer shirts with roll-up sleeve tabs for flexibility. Convertible pants with zip-off legs are useful for changing temperatures, as they can be converted to shorts during warmer hours or on the boat, then zip the legs back on for jungle hikes. Choose earth-tone colors such as greens, browns, and grays, which blend in with the environment and attract fewer insects than bright colors.

Rain Jacket and Waterproof Layers
The Amazon experiences frequent rain, so a lightweight, waterproof rain jacket is essential. Choose a jacket made of breathable materials to avoid overheating, and make sure it fits easily into your day bag for quick access during sudden showers. Ponchos are another option for providing adequate coverage while also protecting your backpack and gear. Consider waterproof overpants as an additional layer of protection to keep you dry on longer hikes or during wet activities.

Insect-Repellant Clothing
Mosquitoes and other insects abound in the Amazon, so insect-repellent clothing is an excellent choice for additional protection. Many outdoor brands sell shirts, pants, and socks treated with permethrin, an insect repellent that lasts through multiple washes. While insect-repellent clothing does not eliminate the need for bug spray, it can add another layer of protection against bites. Look for insect repellent clothing, particularly for evening excursions when insects are most active.

Sturdy, Waterproof Footwear

The Amazon's terrain ranges from muddy trails to riverbanks and boat decks, making footwear essential. A pair of durable, waterproof hiking shoes or boots with good traction will keep your feet safe and provide support on uneven terrain. Lightweight, breathable boots are ideal for keeping your feet comfortable on hikes, and waterproofing keeps them from getting wet. Some travelers bring a pair of quick-drying sandals for activities on the boat or short walks on dry land. Avoid heavy boots, which can be cumbersome in the humid environment, and make sure to break in your shoes before the trip to prevent blisters.

Wide-Brimmed Hat and Sunglasses

Because of its proximity to the equator, the Amazon receives a lot of sun, so bring a wide-brimmed hat to protect your face, neck, and ears. A hat with a chin strap is useful because it keeps you secure on boat rides and windy days. Sunglasses with UV protection are also essential for protecting your eyes from the sun's glare, particularly on open water. Polarized lenses reduce reflections, making it easier to see wildlife on the water's surface.

Multipurpose Scarf or Buff

A lightweight, multipurpose scarf or buff is a useful addition to your Amazon wardrobe. Use it to protect your neck from sunburn, keep sweat out of your eyes, or cover your face for extra dust and insect protection. Buffs are also useful for early morning boat rides, providing an extra layer of warmth when temperatures are cooler. Quick-drying materials are ideal because you may use your scarf or buff several times during the day.

Socks and Underwear Designed for Humid Climates

Moisture-wicking socks and underwear made of synthetic blends or merino wool are essential for comfort in the Amazon's humid climate. Regular cotton socks and underwear can trap moisture, causing discomfort and possible skin irritation. Look for quick-drying, breathable options that will keep you comfortable on hikes and boat rides. Some travelers find it useful to bring extra pairs because humid weather can make it difficult to dry items quickly.

Daypack with Waterproof Cover

A small, comfortable day pack is ideal for carrying items such as a water bottle, insect repellent, camera, and rain gear. Choose a backpack with padded shoulder straps and ventilation to keep your back cool. Many day packs include a built-in waterproof cover, which is useful during unexpected rain showers. If yours does not have one, you should consider purchasing a separate rain cover to keep your belongings dry.

Optional: gaiters or waterproof leggings.

If you intend to hike through deep mud or waterlogged trails, bring gaiters or waterproof leggings. Gaiters fit around your boots and extend up your calves, keeping mud, water, and insects out. While not required for all travelers, they are a useful addition for those planning longer hikes through wet areas.

Packing these clothing and gear essentials will keep you comfortable, safe, and prepared for any conditions the Amazon may throw at you. By emphasizing moisture-wicking, quick-drying materials and versatile, protective gear, you'll be well-equipped to fully enjoy your Amazon experience, rain or shine.

Tech and Photography Equipment for the Amazon

Capturing the Amazon's vast landscapes, exotic wildlife, and vibrant culture can be a highlight of your journey, but it's essential to bring the right tech and photography equipment to make the most of this experience. The Amazon's humid climate, frequent rain, and remote setting pose unique challenges, so careful planning and packing are essential to protect your gear and optimize your photography. Here's a guide to the best tech and photography equipment to bring along and tips to keep it safe and functional.

Camera and Lenses

If photography is a top priority, a DSLR or mirrorless camera with a versatile zoom lens (such as a 70-300mm or 100-400mm) is ideal for capturing both expansive landscapes and distant wildlife. A zoom lens lets you photograph animals from a safe distance without disturbing them, which is especially useful in the Amazon, where wildlife can be elusive or camouflaged. Furthermore, a wide-angle lens (such as a 16-35mm) is ideal for photographing expansive rainforest views, river scenes, and night skies.

If you're a casual photographer or want to keep your setup light, a high-quality compact camera or even a smartphone with a good zoom lens can produce impressive results. Newer smartphones have powerful cameras with features like night mode, portrait mode, and 4K video recording, making them versatile and portable.

Waterproof Action Camera

A waterproof action camera, such as a GoPro, is an excellent choice for documenting the Amazon's wet and adventurous landscapes. Action cameras are waterproof, durable, and compact, making them suitable for river excursions, kayaking, and swimming. Most models also have excellent video stabilization, making them ideal for capturing smooth, high-quality footage while boating or hiking. If you plan to use the camera on the water, bring extra batteries and a floatation accessory.

Binoculars

Binoculars, while not cameras, are essential tools for spotting wildlife in the Amazon, where many animals hide in the dense forest or high in the canopy. A compact pair of binoculars with at least 8x magnification will help you spot birds, monkeys, and other elusive animals. Some binoculars are water-resistant, which is an important feature to look for given the Amazon's rainy climate.

Waterproof cases and dry bags

Humidity and rain can quickly damage electronics, so waterproofing is essential. Bring waterproof cases or dry bags for all of your tech devices, including your camera, smartphone, and any accessories. If your camera is not waterproof, consider purchasing a waterproof housing designed specifically for your model. For added protection, place silica gel packets inside your dry bags to absorb excess moisture, which is especially useful in high-humidity environments such as the Amazon.

Portable Power Bank with Solar Charger

Access to power is limited in remote areas, and some boats may not have regular charging options. A high-capacity power bank with multiple USB ports keeps your camera, phone, and other electronics charged during multi-day trips. Some travelers also bring a solar charger, which can provide an environmentally friendly and dependable power source in sunny weather. Look for solar chargers that are lightweight and compact, and can be attached to your backpack or set up during breaks to charge your devices while on the go.

Extra Memory Cards and Batteries

With the Amazon's spectacular scenery and abundant wildlife, it's easy to take hundreds of photos per day. Bring multiple memory cards to avoid running out of storage, especially if you intend to shoot in RAW format for higher-quality results. Also, bring extra batteries for your camera, as using zoom lenses, video recording, or image stabilization can drain batteries faster than usual. In a humid environment like the Amazon, rechargeable batteries can be more dependable than single-use batteries.

Compact tripod or monopod

A compact, lightweight tripod or monopod is ideal for low-light photography, night shots, and recording stable video footage. In the Amazon, you might find yourself photographing in low-light conditions beneath the forest canopy or on nighttime excursions. A small tripod can also be useful for long-exposure shots of rivers or stars, whereas a monopod provides greater mobility on hikes. Look for a tripod with flexible legs that can be used on uneven surfaces, such as jungle trails.

Lens Cleaning Kit

With frequent rain and high humidity, your lenses are prone to collecting moisture, smudges, and even mud during excursions. A portable lens cleaning kit, which includes a microfiber cloth, lens cleaning solution, and a brush, is essential for maintaining image clarity. If your lens fogs up due to humidity, allow it to adjust to the outdoor temperature before cleaning to prevent streaking. Always clean lenses carefully to avoid scratches, especially when handling them in damp conditions.

Protective Backpack or Camera Bag

A durable, waterproof backpack or dedicated camera bag with padded compartments will keep your gear safe from bumps and moisture. To protect against sudden downpours, look for a weather-sealed bag or one with a built-in rain cover. A backpack with compartments for tech equipment keeps your camera, lenses, and other accessories organized and easily accessible while you're on the go. Some travelers prefer side-access bags, which allow them to quickly reach their cameras when wildlife or scenic views appear unexpectedly.

Additional Accessories

Consider bringing a few extra accessories that can help you capture the Amazon effectively:

Polarizing Filter: This can help reduce glare from water while also enhancing the color of the forest canopy and sky, resulting in more vibrant and clear images.

Strap or Harness: A strong camera strap or harness will keep your camera secure while also providing easy access. Choose a weather-resistant strap to increase durability.

Backup Phone Charger Cable: Due to humidity and frequent use, cables can wear out quickly. A backup charging cable will ensure that you never lose power.

A final word on protecting gear.
Remember that the Amazon's environment can be difficult for electronics, with high humidity, unexpected rain, and occasional encounters with mud or dust. When changing lenses or memory cards, avoid doing so in open, wet conditions. When not in use, keep gear in a dry bag or case. To avoid damage, check your equipment for moisture buildup on a regular basis and clean it with a microfiber cloth.

With the right technology and photography equipment, you'll be well-equipped to capture the beauty of the Amazon and keep the memories of your adventure for years to come. Focusing on weatherproofing, power backups, and essential accessories will allow you to confidently navigate the unique challenges of this stunning region.

Items to Keep You Healthy and Prepared

Staying healthy and prepared in the Amazon requires attention to the tropical climate, potential health risks, and the availability of basic services in remote areas. Bringing the right items will help you manage common issues like insect bites, dehydration, or sudden changes in weather, ensuring a safe and enjoyable journey. Here's a guide to the essentials you'll need to stay healthy and prepared for any situation the Amazon might present.

Insect Repellent with DEET or Picaridin
Mosquitoes and other insects abound in the Amazon, and some can transmit diseases such as malaria and dengue fever. To avoid bites, use a powerful insect repellent containing DEET or picaridin. Apply generously, especially at dawn and dusk, when mosquitos are most active. Consider using it in conjunction with insect repellent or spraying your garments with permethrin before to your vacation. Remember to reapply after exercising or swimming.

Antimalarial Medication
If your schedule involves malaria-risk locations, speak with a healthcare expert regarding antimalarial medicine. To ensure complete safety, follow

the specified course of action both before and after your travel. Be aware of any potential side effects and follow your doctor's instructions to reduce discomfort. Antimalarial tablets are one of the most effective ways to protect oneself, but they should always be used in conjunction with other mosquito protection methods.

Rehydration salts and electrolyte tablets

The Amazon's hot and humid atmosphere can produce dehydration faster than expected, particularly during treks or other vigorous activities. Rehydration salts or electrolyte tablets are a practical way to replenish lost fluids and minerals. Dissolve these in water whenever you feel excessively hot or tired, especially if you're sweating profusely. These packets are lightweight and portable, making them an ideal addition to any travel health kit.

First Aid Kit

A comprehensive first aid bag is crucial for dealing with minor accidents and illnesses when medical services are far away. Include sticky bandages, antiseptic wipes, gauze, and adhesive tape to repair minor cuts and scrapes that can occur on jungle hikes. Other necessary items include pain medicines (such as ibuprofen or acetaminophen), anti-diarrheal medication, and antihistamines for allergic responses. Tweezers, scissors, and blister treatment are all useful additions. Customize the package to your specific needs, especially if you have known allergies or medical issues.

Anti-Diarrheal Medication And Probiotics

Travelers' diarrhea is a typical occurrence in remote areas due to unfamiliar diet or water. Bring an anti-diarrheal drug, such as loperamide, to treat symptoms if they occur. Including probiotics in your regular routine before and during your vacation can also assist to improve gut health and reduce susceptibility to stomach problems. Keep any medication in a waterproof bag to preserve it from dampness.

Biodegradable soap and hand sanitizer

During some excursions in the Amazon, access to clean water and soap may be restricted, so pack a small bottle of biodegradable soap to wash your hands, dishes, and personal items. Hand sanitizer containing at least

60% alcohol is also required to keep your hands clean when water is unavailable, particularly before meals or after handling animals, plants, or soil. These things will help to lower the risk of infection and promote basic hygiene.

Sun Protection: SPF 50+ Sunscreen and SPF lip balm
The Amazon's proximity to the equator results in strong solar exposure, even when the skies are gloomy. Bring a broad-spectrum sunscreen with SPF 50+ and use it freely and frequently, especially on high-exposure regions such as your face, neck, and arms. A lip balm with SPF protection is also recommended to avoid chapped or burnt lips. Reapply both throughout the day, particularly after sweating, swimming, or cleaning your face.

Personal Water Filter or Purification Tablets.
While bottled water is typically provided on Amazon cruises, it is advisable to have a personal water filter or purification tablets, especially if you will be traveling to more remote places. A portable water filter bottle is practical and guarantees that you always have access to healthy drinking water. Purification tablets are a lightweight backup alternative that may be conveniently carried in your backpack and used in the event of an emergency or unexpected stop.

Personal medications and copies of prescriptions.
If you take any regular prescriptions, bring enough for the entire trip, plus a few extra days in case of delays. Access to pharmacies and medical facilities is limited in isolated places, so bring everything you need with you. Store drugs in a waterproof bag to protect them from humidity, and keep a list of vital medications with generic names in case you need replacements. If your medications require refrigeration, contact your cruise operator ahead of time to make arrangements.

Antihistamines and Allergy Relief
Even if you have no known allergies, coming into contact with new plants, animals, or insects in the Amazon can cause unanticipated allergic reactions. Over-the-counter antihistamines, such as loratadine or cetirizine, can help with itching, sneezing, and swelling. If you have severe allergies,

pack an epinephrine injector (EpiPen) and notify your guide or travel companions of its use.

Talcum Powder or Anti-Chafe Cream
The intense humidity in the Amazon can cause chafing, especially on lengthy excursions or when sweating significantly. A tiny jar of talcum powder or anti-chafing cream reduces friction and moisture, making your skin more pleasant and preventing irritation. Apply it on chafing-prone areas like the thighs, underarms, and feet.

Compact towel or cooling towel.
A quick-drying, small towel is useful for wiping away sweat, drying off after a rainstorm, or cooling off on hot days. Cooling towels are meant to retain water and offer a cooling sensation when placed around your neck or forehead, which is very useful in the Amazon heat. Choose a lightweight, packable model that will fit neatly into your daypack.

Emergency whistle and a small flashlight.
An emergency whistle and a compact flashlight are useful additions to your kit, especially if you're traveling into remote areas of the Amazon or going on overnight expeditions. A whistle can help you signal for help if you become separated from your company, while a small, waterproof flashlight or headlamp provides dependable light in the dark. Extra batteries are also recommended because electricity may not be accessible.

Essential Documents: Travel Insurance and Emergency Contacts.
Finally, remember to bring travel insurance that covers medical evacuation, as medical services are scarce in the Amazon. Include emergency contact information for both your insurance provider and your embassy in case of a serious emergency. To keep these documents moisture-free, store them in a waterproof case or ziplock bag.

These products will ensure that you are well-prepared to face the Amazon's unique challenges while being healthy and comfortable throughout your journey. With a well-stocked kit, you'll be able to fully enjoy the Amazon's beauty while minimizing hazards and being proactive about your health.

Packing Light but Smart

Items to Keep You Healthy and Prepared

Staying healthy and prepared in the Amazon requires attention to the tropical climate, potential health risks, and the availability of basic services in remote areas. Bringing the right items will help you manage common issues like insect bites, dehydration, or sudden changes in weather, ensuring a safe and enjoyable journey. Here's a guide to the essentials you'll need to stay healthy and prepared for any situation the Amazon might present.

Insect Repellent with DEET or Picaridin

Mosquitoes and other insects are common in the Amazon, and some can transmit diseases such as malaria and dengue fever. A powerful insect repellent containing DEET or picaridin is essential for limiting bites. Apply liberally, particularly at dawn and dusk, when mosquitoes are most active. Consider wearing bug repellent or spraying your clothing with permethrin before your travel for best effectiveness. Remember to reapply after swimming or sweating.

Antimalarial medication

If your schedule includes places where malaria is a possibility, speak with a doctor about antimalarial medications. To ensure complete protection, follow the specified course before and after your travel. To avoid discomfort, be aware of any potential side effects and adhere to your doctor's advice. Antimalarial tablets are one of the most effective ways to protect yourself, but they must always be taken in conjunction with other mosquito protection measures.

Rehydration Salts and Electrolyte Tablets

The Amazon's hot and humid temperature can lead to dehydration more quickly than expected, particularly during treks or other vigorous activities. Rehydration salts or electrolyte tablets are an effective way to replenish lost fluids and minerals. Dissolve them in water whenever you feel too hot or tired, especially if you're sweating profusely. These packets are lightweight and portable, making them a useful addition to your travel health kit.

First aid kit

A well-stocked first aid bag is vital for treating minor injuries and illnesses when medical services are far away. Include sticky bandages, antiseptic wipes, gauze, and adhesive tape for treating minor cuts and scratches that can occur on jungle hikes. Pain remedies (such as ibuprofen or acetaminophen), anti-diarrheal medications, and antihistamines for allergic reactions are also essential. Tweezers, scissors, and blister therapy are all beneficial extras. Customize the kit to your specific requirements, especially if you have known allergies or medical issues.

Anti-diarrheal medications and probiotics

Travelers' diarrhea is a typical problem in remote areas because of unfamiliar diet or water. Bring anti-diarrheal medication, such as loperamide, to treat symptoms if they occur. Including probiotics in your regular routine before and during your vacation can also aid by improving gut health and lowering your risk of stomach difficulties. To protect medication from dampness, store it in a waterproof bag.

Biodegradable soap and hand sanitizer.

During certain excursions in the Amazon, access to clean water and soap may be restricted, so pack a small bottle of biodegradable soap to clean your hands, dishes, and personal items. Hand sanitizer with at least 60% alcohol is also necessary for keeping your hands clean when water is not accessible, particularly before meals or after handling animals, plants, or soil. These things will help to lower the risk of illness while also maintaining basic hygiene.

Sun Protection: SPF 50+ sunscreen and SPF lip balm.

Because of its proximity to the equator, the Amazon receives a lot of sun, even on cloudy days. Bring a broad-spectrum sunscreen with SPF 50+ and use liberally and frequently, especially on high-exposure regions like your face, neck, and arms. A lip balm with SPF is also recommended to prevent chapped or burnt lips. Reapply both throughout the day, especially if you sweat, swim, or wipe your face.

Personal water filter or purification tablets

While bottled water is normally given on Amazon cruises, it's a good idea to bring your own water filter or purification tablets, especially if you'll be traveling to more remote locations. A portable water filter bottle is practical and guarantees that you always have safe drinking water. Purification tablets are a lightweight backup alternative that can be carried in your backpack and used in the event of an emergency or unexpected stop.

Personal medications, as well as prescription copies
If you take any regular prescriptions, bring enough to last the entire trip, plus a few days in case of delays. Access to pharmacies and medical facilities is restricted in isolated places, so come prepared. Store drugs in a waterproof bag to protect them from dampness, and compile a list of vital medications with generic names in case you need to replace any. If your medications require refrigeration, contact your cruise line in advance to make preparations.

Antihistamines and Allergy Relief
Even if you have no known allergies, encountering new plants, animals, or insects in the Amazon can cause unexpected allergic reactions. Itching, sneezing, and swelling can be relieved with over-the-counter antihistamines such as cetirizine or loratadine. If you have severe allergies, pack an epinephrine injector (EpiPen) and explain to your guide or travel partners how to use it.

Talcum Powder or Anti-chafing Cream
Chafing can occur due to the Amazon's extreme humidity, particularly during long excursions or heavy sweating. A tiny jar of talcum powder or anti-chafing lotion reduces friction and moisture, keeping your skin comfortable and avoiding irritation. Apply it to common chafing areas, such as the thighs, underarms, and feet.

Compact or cooling towel
A quick-dry, compact towel is ideal for wiping away sweat, drying off after a shower, or cooling off on hot days. Cooling towels are intended to retain water and offer a cooling effect when wrapped around your neck or forehead, which can be very useful in the Amazon heat. Choose a lightweight, packable model that will fit neatly into your day bag.

Emergency whistle and a little flashlight

An emergency whistle and a compact flashlight are useful additions to your kit, especially if you're traveling through remote areas of the Amazon or going on overnight expeditions. If you become separated from your party, a whistle can help you signal for aid, and a compact, waterproof flashlight or headlamp will provide you with reliable light in the dark. Extra batteries are also recommended in case electricity is unavailable.

Essential Documents: Travel Insurance and Emergency Contacts

Finally, keep in mind that medical services in the Amazon are limited. Carry travel insurance that includes medical evacuation. Include emergency contact information for both your insurance provider and your embassy in the event of a serious emergency. To prevent moisture damage, store these documents in a waterproof case or ziplock bag.

These goods will ensure that you are well equipped to face the Amazon's unique challenges, keeping you healthy and comfortable throughout your journey. With a well-stocked kit, you'll be able to fully appreciate the Amazon's beauty while limiting hazards and being proactive about your health.

CHAPTER 5

EXPLORING THE FLORA AND FAUNA OF THE AMAZON

Biodiversity Hotspots to Watch For

The Amazon rainforest is renowned for its staggering biodiversity, often described as one of the most complex and vibrant ecosystems on Earth. As a traveler, exploring this rich natural world is one of the highlights of an Amazon River adventure. Certain areas, known as biodiversity hotspots, are particularly abundant in flora and fauna, offering some of the best opportunities for wildlife observation and ecological discovery. Here are some of the most fascinating biodiversity hotspots to look out for during your Amazon journey, along with tips to enhance your experience while keeping safety and respect for the environment in mind.

1. Pacaya-Samiria National Reserve (Peru)

Pacaya-Samiria, one of Peru's largest protected areas, is nicknamed the "Jungle of Mirrors" because of its vast floodplains and mirrored streams. Pacaya-Samiria's flooded woodlands provide a unique environment for a diverse range of species. Pink river dolphins, gigantic otters, manatees, and different monkey species, such as the red howler and spider monkeys, are among the Amazon's emblematic animals. Birdwatchers will appreciate witnessing red macaws, hoatzins, and bright kingfishers flitting along the shoreline.

Tip: Boat cruises in Pacaya-Samiria are common and allow you to get up close to wildlife while limiting your impact on their environments. Be cautious on water-based adventures, as the damp environment might conceal hazards. Follow your guide's advise and remain a safe distance from animals like caimans, which live in the reserve's rivers and streams.

2. Yasuni National Park, Ecuador.

Yasuni National Park is one of the world's most biologically varied places, home to a staggering number of species, many of which are unique to the region. Yasuni, located at the junction of the Amazon Basin and the Andes, is home to lush forests and waterways, as well as distinctive clay licks where animals assemble to eat minerals. These clay licks are great places to watch wildlife, including parrots, peccaries, and even jaguars, who are drawn to the clay for its purifying powers.

Image showing Giant Anaconda, Yasuni national park, Ecuador

Tip: Yasuni's clay licks attract animals at specified times, usually in the morning, so plan accordingly. Binoculars or a zoom lens are useful for studying animals without disturbing them, as it is critical to maintain a respectful distance to avoid stressing or disrupting their activity.

3. Mamirauá Sustainable Development Reserve (Brazil).

Mamirauá Reserve, located in the Brazilian Amazon, is well-known for its sustainable conservation efforts and distinctive flooded woods. During the high-water season, considerable areas of the forest are submerged, forming an aquatic ecosystem excellent for viewing river dolphins, pirarucu (one of the world's largest freshwater fish), and a variety of bird species. The reserve also houses the uncommon and endangered uakari monkey, which is distinguished by its red face and short tail, as well as sloths and other reptiles.

Tip: Mamirauá allows visitors to stay in eco-lodges maintained by local communities, which enhances the experience while promoting sustainable tourism. Caution is suggested when investigating flooded regions, since deep waters conceal buried plants and debris, which might pose a risk. When on small boats, always wear a life jacket and pay strict attention to your guide's directions.

4. Tambopata National Reserve (Peru).

Tambopata, known for its abundant macaw population, is a popular destination for birdwatchers and wildlife enthusiasts. The area is well-known for its vivid macaw clay licks, where visitors may see hundreds of macaws, parrots, and parakeets feeding on mineral-rich clay. Tambopata is also home to mammals such as jaguars, tapirs, and capybaras, as well as reptiles and amphibians that thrive in the area's diverse environments.

Tip: To enhance your chances of seeing macaws at the clay licks, go early in the morning. Prepare for peaceful observation, since noise and unexpected movements may scare the birds away. Wearing neutral-colored clothing allows you to blend in with the surroundings and avoid disturbing the animals.

5. Madidi National Park (Bolivia)

Madidi National Park is a pristine area that includes lowland rainforests, Andean foothills, and cloud forests, resulting in a mosaic of ecosystems that support an astonishing diversity of species. Madidi is a birdwatchers' delight, with over 1,000 bird species, including harpy eagles and Andean cock-of-the-rock. In addition to a diverse range of amphibians and butterflies, the park is home to jaguars, pumas, and spectacled bears.

Tip: Exploring Madidi's different terrains may require steep treks and changing weather conditions, therefore strong hiking boots and a rain poncho are recommended. Always maintain a respectful distance from wildlife, particularly larger creatures like as jaguars, and avoid wandering into dense regions without a guide who is knowledgeable with the terrain and animal behavior.

6. Manaus and Meeting of the Waters (Brazil)

The Meeting of the Waters, near Manaus, is an incredible natural phenomena where the Rio Negro and the Solimões River converge and flow side by side without mixing for several miles. This unusual aquatic environment attracts a diverse range of fish and bird species, and visitors frequently see pink and gray river dolphins. The lush waters are also popular fishing spots for piranhas and arapaima.

Tip: Although the Meeting of the Waters is popular and accessible, it is crucial to use caution when observing from boats because currents can be powerful and unpredictable. It's also a great place to observe river dolphins, but remain a safe distance because these creatures shouldn't be disturbed or chased.

7. Manu Biosphere Reserve (Peru).
Manu Biosphere Reserve includes a variety of environments, from lowland rainforests to high-altitude cloud forests, which sustain a diverse range of species. This area is home to gigantic otters, tapirs, monkeys, and more than 15,000 plant species. Manu is known for its diverse bird population, with species such as cock-of-the-rock, blue-headed macaws, and oropendolas filling the canopy with their colors and noises.

Manu's rainforest can be difficult to explore due to its density, thus a knowledgeable guide is essential here. Carry a headlamp for nighttime exploring, since Manu's diversity comes to life after dark, with sightings of nocturnal species such as kinkajous, bats, and numerous amphibians.

8. Cuyabeno Wildlife Reserve, Ecuador.
Cuyabeno is a protected area recognized for its diverse aquatic and terrestrial fauna. It is one of the few Amazon regions where visitors can readily see the elusive pink river dolphin. The flooded forests and twisting rivers of Cuyabeno provide ideal habitat for caimans, piranhas, anacondas, and many monkey species, including squirrel monkeys and capuchins. The reserve also boasts an excellent collection of orchids and bromeliads, which contribute to its botanical charm.

Squirrel monkeys

Tip: Given Cuyabeno's swampy terrain, waterproof boots and insect repellant are required. Piranha fishing is popular here, but be cautious and observe all guidelines, as the waters may include concealed predators like as caimans. Observing local restrictions protects both you and the wildlife.

9. Anavilhanas Archipelago (Brazil).

The Anavilhanas Archipelago, located in the Rio Negro, is one of the world's largest river archipelagos, with over 400 islands. Birdwatchers and those interested in exploring Amazon rivers will love this one-of-a-kind riverine scenery. Anavilhanas is home to a variety of fish species, river dolphins, and birds, including the Amazon kingfisher. During the wet season, the forest floods, forming a vast maze of rivers best explored by boat.

Tip: Canoeing in Anavilhanas offers for close encounters with wildlife, but always respect the natural barriers and stay in safe locations to avoid mishaps in the maze-like canals. Pay close attention to your guide's instructions, as some locations may have strong currents or dense foliage that make navigating difficult.

Exploring these Amazon hotspots will lead to amazing interactions with the region's rich vegetation and fauna. To make the most of each trip, listen to your guide's recommendations, respect the fragile ecosystems, and prioritize your own and the wonderful species that inhabits the Amazon.

Iconic Wildlife of the Amazon

The Amazon rainforest is a wildlife enthusiast's dream, teeming with a diverse range of animals that are iconic to this vast region. With its unparalleled biodiversity, the Amazon is home to creatures both large and small, many of which are found nowhere else on Earth. Whether you're observing from a riverboat, trekking through the dense jungle, or taking part in a guided night walk, spotting these creatures can be one of the most thrilling parts of your journey. Here's a guide to the most iconic wildlife of the Amazon and tips for seeing them safely and responsibly.

1. Jaguar (Panthera onca)
The jaguar is the Americas' largest cat and a potent symbol of the Amazon. The jaguar, known for its stealth and strength, is a top predator that contributes significantly to ecosystem equilibrium. Spotting a jaguar in the wild is difficult due to their secretive nature, but the best chances are often found in isolated areas of Peru and Brazil, particularly along riverbanks during the dry season when they come to drink.

Tip: If you happen to observe a jaguar, keep a safe distance and remain quiet to avoid frightening it. Jaguars are solitary animals that might become defensive if they feel threatened.

2. Pink River Dolphins (Inia geoffrensis)

The pink river dolphin, also known as boto, is one of the Amazon River's most unusual and charismatic species. Unlike marine dolphins, these freshwater dolphins have adapted to the murky waters of the Amazon and are distinguished by their pinkish hue, which grows more vibrant with age. They are quite intelligent and frequently engage amicably with humans, but they should always be respected and observed without intervention.

Avoid tour operators that advocate swimming with dolphins since it can disrupt their normal behavior. Instead, look for ethical trips that prioritize animal observation over direct engagement.

3. Sloth (three- and two-toed)

The sloth, a renowned rainforest emblem known for its leisurely lifestyle and upside-down perches in the trees, moves slowly. The two-toed and three-toed sloths are the most abundant in the Amazon. They spend the majority of their time in the canopy, moving little to preserve energy, making identifying them a difficult but rewarding task.

Tip: Look for sloths during riverboat trips or guided walks led by knowledgeable naturalists who know where they hide. Binoculars can be really useful for seeing them in the trees.

4. Harpy Eagle (Harpia harpyja).

The harpy eagle is one of the world's largest and most powerful eagles, distinguished by its distinctive crest and deadly talons. With a wingspan of up to seven feet, the harpy eagle preys on medium-sized animals such as monkeys and sloths. These raptors prefer dense forest settings, making them more difficult to observe, but they can be seen in well-protected sites like as Peru's Tambopata National Reserve.

Recommendation: If birdwatching is your primary goal, bring a good pair of binoculars and hire an avian-specific guide. The ideal time to spot a harpy eagle is in the early morning or late afternoon, when they are more active.

5. Giant Otters (Pteronura brasiliensis)

Giant otters are gregarious and playful creatures that live in the Amazon River and Lakes. Otters are known for their loud vocalizations and group life, and they are a sight to behold as they glide over the water, chasing fish and communicating with one another. Despite their cute appearance, they are a vulnerable species due to habitat loss and poaching.

When seeing huge otters, keep a reasonable distance and be silent because loud noises might interrupt their communication and activity. Ethical tour providers will make sure that boat trips do not disrupt their natural habitat.

6. Anacondas (Eunectes spp.)

The Amazon Basin's marshes and slow-moving rivers are home to the world's largest and heaviest snake, the green anaconda. Anacondas are feared for their size and strength, yet they are not normally hostile toward humans and prefer to pursue animals such as capybaras, fish, and caimans.

Caution: Spotting an anaconda in the wild should be done from a safe distance, preferably from a boat with an experienced guide who can see any hazards. Never approach or provoke one; they are formidable constrictors.

7. Poison Dart Frog (Dendrobatidae).

Poison dart frogs, with their vibrant, jewel-like colors, are both attractive and dangerous. To protect themselves against predators, these little amphibians produce toxins through their skin. The Amazon's indigenous people have long been aware of these frogs' formidable resistance, and have traditionally used their toxins to coat hunting darts.

Tip: Avoid touching or handling frogs or other amphibians since their skin is sensitive, and some species can be hazardous. Admire them from a safe distance, and use a zoom lens to capture close-up shots.

8. Toucans and macaws

Toucans and macaws are among the most bright and colorful birds in the Amazon, distinguished by their huge beaks and eye-catching plumage. Toucans are regularly seen in the higher canopy, while macaws, such as the scarlet and blue-and-yellow macaws, congregate around clay licks to absorb mineral-rich clay.

Bring binoculars and leave early in the morning for the finest birdwatching chances. Clay licks are ideal for photographing macaws in large numbers.

9. Caiman (Caimaninae)

Caimans are relatives of alligators and can be found in the Amazon's rivers, lakes, and marshes. The black caiman, the largest species, can reach 20 feet and is a strong apex predator. While they are normally not aggressive toward humans until attacked, it is vital to exercise caution when approaching them, particularly at night.

Caution: When spotting caimans, always follow your guide's safety precautions, especially at night. Flash photography can shock and irritate these creatures, so avoid it unless approved by your guide.

Exploring the Amazon's famed animals is awe-inspiring, highlighting the planet's immense biodiversity. By adopting ethical standards and respecting these creatures' native habitats, you may help to preserve the Amazon's fragile environment while having a once-in-a-lifetime adventure.

Rare Plant Species and Medicinal Uses

The Amazon rainforest is not only home to an incredible array of wildlife but also hosts a rich diversity of plant life, much of which holds significant medicinal value. Indigenous communities have long harnessed the healing properties of these plants, and modern research has only begun to uncover the potential of these natural remedies. Understanding the rare plant species of the Amazon and their traditional medicinal uses can provide deeper insight into the rainforest's importance and the need to preserve it. Here are some of the most remarkable plant species and their uses, as well as recommendations and cautions for exploring them.

1. Ayahuasca (Banisteriopsis caapi and Psychotria viridis)
Ayahuasca is a strong brew derived from the Banisteriopsis caapi vine and Psychotria viridis leaves. Indigenous Amazonian communities have utilized it for generations in spiritual and therapeutic rites. The mixture has strong hallucinogenic effects and is thought to provide psychological insights, cure emotional damage, and connect people to the spiritual world.

Ayahuasca should only be drunk in the presence of expert shamans in regulated ritual settings. If you want to participate in an ayahuasca ceremony, look for trustworthy centers that value safety, ethics, and respect for indigenous traditions. Be aware of the potential risks, since the experience can be intense and not appropriate for everyone.

2. Cat's Claw (Uncaria Tomentosa)

Cat's Claw is a vine endemic to the Amazon notable for its claw-shaped thorns. Traditionally, indigenous people have utilized its bark and roots to treat a wide range of diseases, including inflammation, digestive problems, and joint discomfort. Modern research reveals that Cat's Claw contains anti-inflammatory and immune-boosting qualities, making it a popular natural supplement.

Caution: While Cat's Claw is usually considered safe when used correctly, pregnant or nursing women should avoid it owing to potential negative effects. Always contact with your doctor before using it as a treatment, especially if you have pre-existing health conditions or are using drugs.

3. Cinchona (Cinchona spp.)

Cinchona trees, noted for their medicinal bark, are well-known as the original source of quinine, a chemical used to cure malaria for centuries. The discovery of quinine transformed the treatment of this mosquito-borne

97

disease, and it is still a valuable antimalarial medicine today. Cinchona bark tea was utilized by indigenous Amazonian tribes to treat fevers and other diseases.

Dried Cinchona

While quinine from cinchona has saved lives, it should only be administered in regulated medical settings due to its powerful effects. Modern antimalarial drugs are frequently favored over raw cinchona bark due to safety and efficacy.

4. Sacha Inchi (Plukenetia Volubilis)

Sacha Inchi, commonly known as Inca peanut, is a shrub with star-shaped seed pods. The seeds, which are high in omega-3 fatty acids, protein, and antioxidants, are considered a superfood. Sacha Inchi has long been consumed by indigenous populations due to its nutritional qualities, and it is now widely used in oils, powders, and snacks. The plant's anti-inflammatory effects are good to heart health and overall well-being.

Tip: Sacha Inchi is readily accessible at health food stores, but if you come across it when shopping on Amazon, you may be able to find local, fresh versions with even more nutritional benefits. To promote responsible harvesting techniques, ensure that any plant-based products you eat are derived sustainably.

5. Guaraná (Paullinia Cupana)

Guaraná is a climbing plant that produces caffeine-rich seeds that are commonly used as a stimulant in energy drinks and supplements. Guaraná has long been utilized by indigenous tribes to combat weariness, boost focus, and increase general stamina. It is also recognized for its antioxidant capabilities, which can help fight oxidative stress in the body.

Guaraná is a natural energy booster, but it should be used in moderation due to its high caffeine concentration, which can cause negative effects such as increased heart rate, anxiety, or insomnia. Caffeine-sensitive people and those with cardiac issues should exercise caution.

6. Uña de Gato (uncaria guianensis)
Uña de Gato, often known as "Cat's Claw," has similar health advantages to Uncaria tomentosa, although being a distinct species. Amazonian healers have traditionally utilized it to boost their immune systems and reduce inflammation. Compounds in Uña de Gato may support the immune system and treat illnesses like arthritis and gastrointestinal ailments, according to recent studies.

Tip: When looking for Cat's Claw supplements, examine the source and quality to guarantee the product was harvested ethically and sustainably. Ethical harvesting benefits local populations and aids to the preservation of Amazonian biodiversity.

7. Copaiba (copaifera spp.)
Copaiba oil is derived from the resin of the Copaifera tree and is highly prized for its anti-inflammatory and antibacterial effects. Copaiba oil has long been used topically by indigenous people to treat wounds, skin ailments, and bug bites. It is also used internally to promote respiratory and digestive health.

Copaiba oil should be used with caution, particularly when consumed. Consult a healthcare physician or an expert herbalist before using it internally, as it might interfere with drugs or cause negative effects if used incorrectly.

8. Brazil Nut Tree (Bertholletia Excelsa)

Brazil nut trees are among the most significant ecological and commercial species in the Amazon. Brazil nuts are high in selenium, a vital mineral with antioxidant qualities that promote thyroid function and immunological health. The trees are large and play an important part in the rainforest environment by providing food and shelter for a variety of creatures.

Recommendation: Brazil nuts are a nutritious snack, but moderation is essential due to their high selenium content. Overconsumption can cause selenium toxicity. Look for responsibly sourced Brazil nuts to help preserve the rainforest and support local populations that rely on this resource for a living.

9. Dragon's Blood (Croton Lechleri)

Dragon's blood is a dark red resin derived from the bark of the Croton lechleri tree. This resin has long been utilized for its antibacterial, anti-inflammatory, and wound healing qualities. Indigenous healers frequently use it to make salves to treat cuts, insect bites, and other skin problems. Dragon's Blood is also being investigated for its possible benefits in gastrointestinal health due to its protective components.

Tip: Before using Dragon's Blood for any skin treatment, test a tiny area to ensure there are no adverse reactions. To safeguard trees and biodiversity, buy from reliable vendors that use ethical harvesting procedures.

Exploring the Amazon's rare plant species and therapeutic uses serves as a reminder of the rainforest's unparalleled worth to indigenous knowledge and world health. However, always approach these potent plants with respect and caution, and consult local experts or healthcare specialists as needed. By respecting and preserving these species and their ecosystems, future generations will be able to learn from the Amazon's remarkable biodiversity.

Guided Excursions and Nature Walks

Guided excursions and nature walks are some of the most enriching activities available to travelers in the Amazon, offering firsthand exposure to the rainforest's unparalleled biodiversity and cultural heritage. These outings provide a unique way to witness the intricate relationships within the ecosystem and learn from experts who have an intimate understanding of the forest's wonders. Whether you're a seasoned explorer or a first-time visitor, guided excursions are essential to fully appreciating the Amazon and ensuring a safe, informative journey.

Guided excursions are typically led by experienced naturalists, biologists, or local guides who are well-versed in the region's flora, fauna, and ecological balance. Their knowledge is invaluable, transforming a simple walk through the jungle into an educational experience. These guides can point out well-camouflaged wildlife, identify unusual plants, and share traditional stories or cultural uses for natural resources. Having a knowledgeable guide also improves your safety because they can help you navigate the dense terrain, identify potential hazards, and provide safety tips such as avoiding certain plants or knowing how to react to wildlife encounters.

Nature walks frequently begin in the early morning or late afternoon, when the forest is most active. Early morning excursions are especially rewarding because birds, monkeys, and other wildlife are more visible in the cooler hours. These walks allow you to hear the rainforest's symphony of sounds, including chirping birds, buzzing insects, and distant howler monkey calls. A guided walk at dawn can be a magical experience, with mist rising from the forest floor and soft light filtering through the canopy, creating an ethereal environment. Night walks, on the other hand, show a completely different side of the Amazon, with nocturnal creatures such as frogs, spiders, and bats coming to life. Guides, armed with flashlights or headlamps, lead groups into the darkness to locate animals that are hidden during the day, adding a sense of adventure and excitement.

One of the most significant advantages of guided excursions is the opportunity to see the rainforest's delicate web of life up close. Guides can explain how trees, plants, and animals work together to keep the ecosystem balanced, from the massive kapok trees that tower over the canopy to the ants that keep the forest floor healthy. This detailed knowledge deepens your understanding of the rainforest's complexity and fosters a greater appreciation for conservation efforts.

Nature walks also allow you to learn about the medicinal and cultural applications of different plants. Guides frequently tell stories about how indigenous communities have used specific plants for centuries, whether for food, medicine, or ritual. This insight emphasizes the importance of preserving not only the Amazon's biodiversity, but also the traditional knowledge held by its indigenous people. For example, guides may point out a curare vine, which is used as a natural anesthetic and in traditional hunting practices, or the bark of a cinchona tree, which is famous for being the original source of quinine, a malaria treatment.

When going on guided nature walks, dress appropriately for the rainforest environment. Lightweight, long-sleeved clothing and pants protect against the sun and insect bites, while sturdy, waterproof footwear is essential for navigating muddy trails or wading through shallow waters. A hat and sunglasses can provide extra sun protection, and a high-quality insect repellent will keep mosquitoes at bay. Carrying a reusable water bottle filled with purified water will keep you hydrated throughout your walk, especially during the more humid parts of the day.

Guided nature walks provide an excellent opportunity for photographers to capture the beauty of the rainforest. The guides know the best spots for sightings and can help you position yourself for the best lighting and angles. However, keep in mind that the primary goal should be to observe and respect wildlife, so avoid using flash photography, which can startle animals and disrupt their natural behavior. A good zoom lens will enable you to take impressive shots from a distance, capturing details without invading the wildlife's space.

When planning a guided tour, select operators who value responsible and sustainable tourism practices. Ethical operators frequently collaborate with local communities and employ indigenous guides, who share their invaluable knowledge. Supporting these tours promotes conservation and ensures that tourism's economic benefits reach local communities, instilling a sense of ownership and commitment to rainforest preservation.

If you want a more immersive experience, consider multi-day trips that include camping or stays in eco-lodges deep in the forest. These experiences allow you to observe how the Amazon changes from dawn to dusk and throughout the night, providing a more complete understanding of the forest's rhythms. While these extended excursions provide unparalleled intimacy with the environment, they necessitate more planning, such as packing biodegradable toiletries and a small first-aid kit.

Guided excursions and nature walks are essential for having an authentic and safe experience in the Amazon. With the assistance of experienced guides, you'll discover insights that will deepen your understanding of this amazing environment and the critical need to protect it. By engaging in these activities responsibly and with respect for local customs and wildlife, you help to promote sustainable tourism that protects and celebrates the Amazon's unique biodiversity.

Tips for Ethical Wildlife Viewing

Experiencing the Amazon's extraordinary wildlife up close is a privilege, but it comes with a responsibility to view animals ethically and ensure their habitats remain undisturbed. Ethical wildlife viewing promotes respect for the animals and their environment, supporting conservation efforts while providing an unforgettable experience. Here are some essential tips to help you engage in wildlife viewing that is both respectful and enriching.

Maintain a Safe and Respectful Distance
One of the most important principles of ethical wildlife viewing is to keep a safe distance from the animals. While it may be tempting to get closer for a better look or a photograph, doing so can stress wildlife, disrupt their natural behavior, and even elicit defensive responses. Using binoculars or a camera with a zoom lens, you can observe and photograph wildlife from a distance without causing them distress. Always listen to your guide's advice on how close is safe and appropriate to observe specific animals.

Avoid feeding wildlife.
Feeding wildlife is harmful to both the animals and the environment. When animals become accustomed to human food, it can result in nutritional deficiencies, behavioral changes, and an increased reliance on human interactions. Some animals may become aggressive in their pursuit of food, endangering both themselves and visitors. Ethical wildlife viewing entails

allowing animals to find their own food sources while keeping snacks and food items securely stored to avoid attracting animals.

Minimize noise and movement.

Animals in the Amazon are particularly sensitive to loud noises and sudden movements. To ensure a peaceful observation, speak quietly and move slowly. This approach not only reduces stress for wildlife, but it also increases your chances of spotting animals that would otherwise remain hidden. Whether you're on a guided nature walk or observing from a boat, remaining calm and quiet is critical for ethical wildlife viewing.

Don't touch or interact with wildlife.

While it may appear harmless to reach out and touch a sloth hanging nearby or attempt to coax a monkey closer, direct interaction with wildlife can have serious consequences. Touching animals can transmit diseases to and from humans, weaken the animals' natural defense mechanisms, and cause behavioral changes that could endanger them in the future. Ethical viewing focuses on observing and appreciating wildlife without making physical contact.

Stick to the designated paths and areas.

Staying on marked trails and observation points helps to protect the Amazon's fragile ecosystems. Going off-path can disrupt animal habitats, harm plant life, and put you at risk of encountering dangerous wildlife or terrain. Responsible tour operators will plan excursions to reduce environmental impact and encourage visitors to follow local conservation guidelines. Trust your guides and stick to their recommended routes to ensure your and the wildlife's safety.

Use ethical photography practices.

Wildlife photography should prioritize the animal's well-being over the ideal shot. Flash photography, in particular, can startle and disturb animals, particularly nocturnal species with eyes adapted to low light. Instead of using your camera's flash, capture images using natural light or equipment with good low-light capability. Be patient and wait for animals to appear rather than pursuing them, as chasing or cornering wildlife for photos is both unethical and dangerous.

Travel with responsible tour operators.
Choosing a tour operator that prioritizes ethical practices is essential for responsible wildlife viewing. Look for companies that hire local and indigenous guides who understand and respect the environment, support conservation projects, and adhere to wildlife viewing guidelines. Operators who support environmentally friendly practices and collaborate with local communities help to ensure that your presence in the Amazon benefits the region's sustainability.

Limit your group size.
Large gatherings can be noisy and disruptive to wildlife. Smaller tour groups provide a more intimate and less intrusive experience, allowing you to observe animals without causing them stress. Smaller groups are also easier for guides to manage, giving them more control over the group's behavior and ensuring adherence to ethical practices.

Respect wildlife during breeding and feeding periods.
Animals are especially vulnerable during breeding and feeding seasons because they are focused on raising their young or finding food. It is acceptable to observe these activities from a distance, but not to interrupt them. Disturbing an animal during these critical periods can result in abandoned young or missed feeding opportunities, compromising the animal's survival and well-being. A knowledgeable guide will understand the best times and methods for observing wildlife without interfering with these important activities.

Take only memories, leave no trace.
Leave the environment exactly as you found it by not removing any plants, rocks, or other natural items. Even seemingly innocuous actions, such as picking flowers or taking small items as souvenirs, can disrupt the ecosystem. Follow the "Leave No Trace" principle to ensure that your presence does not harm the environment or wildlife.

Educate yourself before and during your trip.
Understanding the behaviors, habitats, and conservation status of the animals you may encounter enriches your experience and fosters a deeper appreciation for wildlife. Take the time to learn about the Amazon's unique ecosystem and the roles that each species plays within it. This awareness

allows you to make more informed decisions during your visit and promotes responsible behavior that benefits conservation.

By following these guidelines, you can have an authentic and respectful wildlife viewing experience while protecting the delicate balance of the Amazon ecosystem. Ethical practices ensure that the rainforest's beauty and biodiversity are preserved for future generations, making your experience not only memorable but also meaningful.

CHAPTER 6

CULTURAL ENCOUNTERS ALONG THE AMAZON RIVER

Indigenous Tribes and Their Traditions

The Amazon River is more than just a natural wonder; it is the lifeblood of countless indigenous tribes who have called its basin home for thousands of years. These tribes, each with their unique traditions and ways of life, represent some of the last connections humanity has to ancient knowledge and practices that have been passed down through countless generations. Encountering these indigenous communities offers travelers an unparalleled opportunity to experience living cultures that are deeply intertwined with the natural environment. To explore the Amazon without acknowledging the people who have shaped and been shaped by this incredible landscape would be to miss an essential part of its story.

The Amazon Basin is home to hundreds of different tribes, each with their own language, customs, and belief systems. The Yanomami are well-known for their intricate communal living structures, known as shabonos, which are circular and made of local materials such as palm leaves and vines. The Yanomami are semi-nomadic and inextricably linked to the forest, relying on it for food, medicine, and shelter. Their traditional way of life involves a delicate balance of hunting, fishing, and sustainable agriculture, and their spiritual practices are based on the belief that all living things have a spirit.

The Tikuna people, one of the largest indigenous groups in the Amazon, have traditions centered on the river itself. The river provides fish, which is the primary source of their diet, as well as water for daily use. One of their most celebrated traditions is the Fiesta de la Moça Nueva (Feast of the New Girl), a rite of passage for young girls transitioning into womanhood. This vibrant ceremony includes singing, dancing, and storytelling, all of which are integral to Tikuna culture. Witnessing or participating in such a tradition provides a deep insight into the Amazon's cultural fabric, emphasizing the value of community and the shared celebration of life's milestones.

The Shipibo-Conibo people, who live primarily in Peru, are known for their intricate art and textiles. The designs frequently incorporate mesmerizing geometric patterns that are not only beautiful but also hold significant meaning. These patterns are thought to represent the shamans' songs and the flow of the Amazon River itself. The Shipibo-Conibo are well-known for their extensive knowledge of medicinal plants, and they use the forest as a living pharmacy. This knowledge is passed down orally from elders to younger generations, preserving traditions and the vital link between people and the environment.

When visiting these communities, it is critical to arrive with respect and an open mind. Indigenous tribes frequently welcome visitors who genuinely want to learn about their way of life and approach their culture with respect. Joining a guided tour led by locals or organizations that collaborate with indigenous groups guarantees that interactions are ethical and beneficial to the community. It is also important to recognize that, while many tribes are willing to share aspects of their culture, others may be more reserved or protective of their privacy, particularly those who have had negative past interactions with outsiders. Always follow your guide's advice on what constitutes respectful behavior, and never impose on private or sacred spaces without permission.

Indigenous traditions in the Amazon frequently emphasize sustainability and the interconnectedness of life. These communities have a wealth of knowledge about the rainforest, which stems from an understanding that environmental health has a direct impact on their own survival. Many tribes practice sustainable slash-and-burn agriculture, which involves leaving small clearings to regenerate naturally. Hunting and fishing practices are typically carried out with great regard for the balance of the ecosystem, ensuring that no species is overharvested. Learning from these practices can teach us valuable lessons about conservation and living in harmony with nature, which is becoming increasingly important in today's world of environmental challenges.

Many indigenous communities in the Amazon face significant challenges, such as deforestation, illegal mining, and outsider encroachment. These threats not only endanger their homes and livelihoods, but they also have the potential to erase irreplaceable cultural knowledge. Supporting eco-tourism that works with indigenous communities can have a significant impact by providing an alternative source of income while also reinforcing the importance of preserving their land and traditions.

Engaging with Amazonian indigenous tribes can be a life-changing experience for travelers. It sheds light on a millennia-old way of life, providing insights into a respectful, reciprocal, and deeply spiritual relationship with nature. However, it is critical to act responsibly. Take the time to learn about the customs before your visit, ask respectful questions, and support initiatives that prioritize these communities' well-being. This will not only enrich your journey, but will also help to preserve the Amazon's cultural heritage, ensuring that these traditions are passed down to future generations.

Festivals and Local Celebrations

The Amazon is not only a treasure trove of natural wonders but also a vibrant tapestry of cultural traditions and festivities. The festivals and local celebrations held along the Amazon River reflect the rich heritage and deep-rooted beliefs of the indigenous and local communities. These celebrations often blend elements of spiritual, social, and environmental significance, showcasing the unique worldview that connects these people to the forest and river. For travelers, witnessing or participating in these festivals offers a rare opportunity to engage deeply with the local culture and witness traditions that have been preserved for generations.

The Feast of Saint John the Baptist (Festa de São João) is widely celebrated in Brazil's Amazonas region. This festival, held on June 24th, combines Catholic and indigenous beliefs by honoring Saint John while also paying homage to water spirits. Celebrations are distinguished by colorful processions, traditional dances, and elaborate costumes. The streets come alive with music, food stalls selling local delicacies like tacacá (tangy shrimp soup), and drumbeats. This festival provides visitors with a sensory experience of Amazonian culture at its most colorful and vibrant. Attending the festival allows you to sample regional cuisine, participate in dances, and watch fireworks illuminate the night sky over the river.

Another notable celebration is the Boi-Bumbá Festival, which is held in Parintins, Brazil, usually in late June. This event is based on Amazonian folklore about a resurrected bull, which has been retold through dance, music, and theater for generations. The festival pits two teams, the Garantido and the Caprichoso, against each other in a complex, high-energy competition. Each team portrays a bull and puts on a spectacular show with colorful costumes, floats, and performances that tell stories about indigenous traditions, nature, and Amazonian mythology. Visitors can buy tickets to see the shows in the massive arena known as the Bumbódromo, which features a captivating blend of dance, song, and storytelling. If you plan to attend, book your accommodations and tickets well in advance, as the festival attracts people from all over the world.

For a more intimate and spiritually significant experience, the Tikuna people celebrate the Feast of the Moça Nova, which marks the coming of age of young girls. This festival commemorates a girl's transition into womanhood and features rituals such as traditional singing, dancing, and elaborate face painting. The entire community gathers for this important rite of passage, fostering a strong sense of community and celebration. While witnessing this event as a visitor requires sensitivity and respect for the community's traditions, attending via invitation or guided cultural tour can provide in-depth insights into the Tikuna people's customs and spiritual beliefs. Always consult with a knowledgeable guide who has built relationships with the locals to ensure that your presence is welcomed and respected.

In Peru, the Yarinacocha Carnival is held in Pucallpa and its surrounding areas. This celebration, which coincides with Carnival in other parts of the world, includes processions, traditional dances, and music that highlight the region's mestizo and indigenous roots. The event also includes water-related activities such as canoe races and water fights, which represent the river's vital role in Amazonian culture. If you're in Peru during Carnival season, going to Pucallpa to see the Yarinacocha Carnival offers a one-of-a-kind experience that combines indigenous and modern festivities.

Participating in these festivals requires a respectful attitude. Always consult with local guides or community leaders who can explain the significance of particular rituals and customs. They can offer advice on appropriate attire, behavior, and how to express gratitude without interfering with sacred practices. Remember that many celebrations incorporate elements of spirituality and cultural pride, so approach photography and recording with caution. Always seek permission before taking photographs, especially during intimate or sacred moments.

When attending these events, travelers should consider sustainability and responsible tourism. Avoid bringing single-use plastics or other items that will contribute to community waste. Participating in or purchasing from local artisans benefits the community while also ensuring that your visit has a positive economic impact. When enjoying traditional food and drinks, look for stalls and vendors that use locally sourced ingredients, as this helps to preserve traditional recipes and promotes sustainable practices in the region.

Those interested in deeper participation in cultural practices should consider attending workshops or community-led activities that frequently accompany major festivals. These may include learning local dances, attempting traditional crafts, or attending storytelling sessions in which local elders share myths and tales passed down through generations. Engaging in these activities not only enhances your experience, but also fosters a meaningful connection with the Amazon's people and traditions.

Attending Amazonian festivals and local celebrations is a unique way to learn about the region's culture and heritage. With respectful participation and the guidance of local experts, these experiences can become treasured memories, revealing the vibrant, enduring spirit of Amazonian communities.

Visiting Local Villages Responsibly

Visiting local villages along the Amazon River is one of the most enriching aspects of any trip to the region. These encounters offer travelers the opportunity to gain insight into the daily life, traditions, and practices of the indigenous communities that have lived in harmony with the rainforest for centuries. However, it's essential to approach these visits with respect, responsibility, and an open mind to ensure that your presence benefits rather than disrupts the community. Here's a comprehensive guide on how to visit local villages responsibly while making your experience truly meaningful.

Engage with Reputable Tour Operators

The first step toward visiting Amazonian villages responsibly is to select a tour operator that values ethical tourism and has established relationships with local communities. Reputable operators collaborate with villages to ensure that visits respect local customs while also contributing to the community's economic well-being. Look for operators that use local guides, who can provide a more in-depth and authentic understanding of the community's culture and history.

Learn about the community before you visit.

Taking the time to learn about the community before you arrive can make your visit more meaningful and respectful. Understanding the fundamentals of the tribe's language, customs, and beliefs demonstrates that you value their culture and are not seeking a superficial experience. For example, understanding that certain gestures or words may have multiple meanings can help you avoid misunderstandings. If your guide provides a briefing prior to your visit, pay close attention and don't be afraid to ask questions about what is and isn't acceptable.

Show respect for traditions and everyday life.

When visiting a village, remember that you are entering someone's home and daily life. Be mindful of local customs, such as how to greet people, dress modestly, and refrain from disrupting daily routines. Simple acts of respect, such as asking permission before taking photos or participating in activities, go a long way toward establishing trust and demonstrating that you are willing to engage with the community on their terms. Some communities may welcome visitors taking photos, while others may consider it intrusive or disrespectful, particularly during sacred rituals or personal moments.

Participate and Support Local Activities.
Many communities host workshops or activities where visitors can learn traditional skills like crafting, cooking, and fishing. Participating in these activities allows you to connect with the locals, learn about their way of life, and help to preserve cultural traditions. Whether you're weaving a basket, trying your hand at pottery, or tasting a traditional dish, participating in these activities helps local artisans and shows you appreciate their work. If the items are available for purchase, consider purchasing directly from the artisans. This not only provides them with income but also helps to maintain their way of life.

Be cautious about gifts and donations.
While it may appear generous to bring gifts or make donations, this should be done carefully to avoid unintended consequences. Giving out gifts, particularly to children, can foster dependency or expectations that all visitors will reciprocate. If you want to help the community, consult your guide or community leaders about the best ways to do so. Donations of practical items, such as school supplies or clothing, are frequently appreciated, but they should be made through established channels to ensure that they reach their intended recipients in a fair and respectful manner.

Respect Personal Space and Privacy.
While you may be curious about how the villagers live, keep in mind that they are not an entertainment exhibit. Avoid peering into people's homes or taking photographs of them without their permission, as this can feel intrusive. It is encouraged to express genuine interest and ask respectful questions, but be aware of any body language or verbal cues that may

indicate discomfort or a desire for privacy. Always approach interactions with humility and gratitude, knowing that you are a guest.

Limit your environmental impact.
The Amazon is not only home to these communities, but it also serves as a vital ecosystem for their survival. When visiting villages, make sure to leave no trace of your visit. This includes taking all of your waste with you, avoiding single-use plastics, and refraining from picking plants or disturbing wildlife. Supporting eco-friendly practices, such as bringing a reusable water bottle and biodegradable toiletries, demonstrates respect for the community's reliance on nature and encourages sustainable tourism.

Avoid making assumptions.
One of the most important aspects of visiting an indigenous village is not to make assumptions or pass judgment. The way of life in these communities may be very different from what you are used to, but that does not diminish its validity or significance. Practices or beliefs that appear unusual to you may have deep cultural or spiritual significance. Accept the opportunity to learn and broaden your perspective, and avoid providing unsolicited advice or comparisons to your own way of life.

Be patient and flexible.
Life in Amazonian villages frequently moves at a different pace than many visitors are used to. Activities may not begin on a set schedule, and conversations or gatherings may last longer than anticipated. Accept the slower pace and use it as an opportunity to completely immerse yourself in the moment. Being patient and adaptable shows respect for the local way of life and allows you to experience the Amazon in its most authentic form.

Leave with more than souvenirs.
Visiting a local village in the Amazon provides a unique opportunity to learn about the deep connection between people and nature, as well as the wisdom and resilience of indigenous cultures. Leave with more than just photographs and handcrafted crafts, but also a better understanding of how these communities coexist with the environment and one another. Share what you've learned with others to raise awareness about the importance of preserving the Amazon's natural and cultural heritage.

Following these guidelines will ensure that your visit to an Amazonian village is respectful, responsible, and rewarding. Engaging thoughtfully and ethically will enrich your experience while also contributing to the well-being of the communities, allowing them to preserve their traditions and protect the valuable ecosystem they call home.

The Amazonian Art and Craft Scene

The Amazonian art and craft scene is as vibrant and diverse as the rainforest itself. Rooted in centuries-old traditions, the artisans of the Amazon use materials found in their natural surroundings to create stunning pieces that are both beautiful and practical. From intricate beadwork and woven baskets to wood carvings and pottery, each item reflects the deep cultural heritage and profound connection these communities have with the environment. For travelers, exploring the art and craft scene is an opportunity to appreciate the craftsmanship, learn about traditional techniques, and support the local economy.

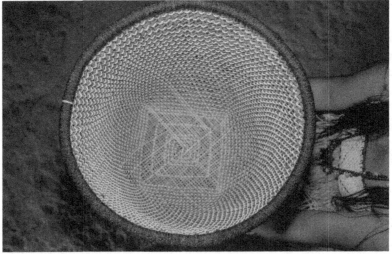

A Deep Connection to Nature and Tradition

The natural world and the indigenous people's cultural beliefs have had a profound influence on Amazonian art. Many of the materials used in crafting come directly from the rainforest, such as palm fibers, seeds, clay, and wood. For example, the vibrant beads used in necklaces and bracelets are frequently made from huayruro seeds, which are known for their bright red and black colors and are thought to bring good luck and protection. The artisans frequently incorporate symbolic meaning into their work, depicting animals, plants, and spiritual elements that are important to their beliefs.

Crafts are more than just decorative items; they are an important part of Amazonian communities' daily lives and traditions. Handwoven baskets, known as cestos, are used to transport fruits, fish, and other goods, whereas pottery is made to store water and cook food. These items' designs are more than just aesthetically pleasing; they tell stories, convey identity, and serve as a form of communication passed down through generations. Because of the skill and care that goes into each piece, Amazonian crafts are a living testament to these communities' rich heritage.

Where to Experience Amazonian Arts and Crafts
Visiting local markets is a great way to get a firsthand look at the art and craft scene. Cities that serve as gateways to the Amazon, such as Iquitos, Manaus, and Leticia, have bustling artisan markets where you can find a variety of handcrafted items. These markets provide a glimpse into the craftsmanship of various indigenous groups, each with their own unique styles and materials. For example, the Shipibo-Conibo people of Peru are well-known for their textiles with intricate geometric patterns that are said to represent the Amazon River's songs and energy flow.

If you're exploring more remote areas or participating in a guided village tour, you might be able to meet artisans in their home communities. This type of encounter provides a better understanding of the time, skill, and cultural significance involved in each craft. It is not uncommon for artisans to tell stories about how they learned their craft from elders or how specific motifs are inspired by local legends or spiritual beliefs. Such interactions offer an invaluable connection to the art and the people who create it.

Tips for Ethical Artisan Support
When purchasing crafts, try to buy directly from artisans or trusted cooperatives whenever possible. This ensures that your money goes directly to the artists and their families, supporting their livelihoods and

preserving the community's cultural heritage. Avoid purchasing items derived from endangered or protected species, such as certain types of wood or animal parts, as they contribute to environmental degradation and illegal trade. Authentic crafts made from sustainable materials, such as palm fibers and non-endangered seeds, are not only beautiful, but also ethical and consistent with responsible tourism practices.

Before making a purchase, inquire about the piece's origin, materials, and techniques. Artisans are often proud to share these details, and your interest shows respect and appreciation for their work. Keep in mind that handmade items may be more expensive than mass-produced items, but this reflects the skill and time required to create them. Purchasing genuine, handcrafted items not only provides unique, meaningful souvenirs, but also supports sustainable practices and local economies.

Workshops and hands-on experiences
If you're looking for more than just crafts, many communities host workshops where visitors can learn traditional techniques and create their own pieces. These experiences give students a hands-on connection to the art form as well as a better understanding of the challenges and dedication required to complete the process. Workshops may include lessons on how to weave baskets, paint traditional patterns, or carve small wooden figures. Participation in such activities benefits the artisans and preserves the knowledge passed down through generations.

Care for Your Amazonian Crafts
Once you've brought your Amazonian crafts home, proper care will ensure they last for years and remind you of your adventure. Natural materials, such as palm fibers and wood, can be sensitive to humidity and temperature fluctuations. Keep these items cool and dry, away from direct sunlight, which can fade colors and weaken fibers over time. If your crafts are made from seeds or other natural materials, dust them gently on a regular basis to keep them looking good and prevent buildup that could cause deterioration.

Recommendations for Travelers
When visiting artisan markets or villages, show respect and curiosity. Take your time learning about the crafts and their significance, and avoid

haggling aggressively. Bargaining, which is common in many parts of the world, can be disrespectful to artisans whose livelihoods rely on their work. If a price feels reasonable and within your budget, consider paying it as a show of support and gratitude for the effort put into creating the piece.

If you are unsure of your home country's customs regulations, exercise caution when making large purchases or bulk purchases. Some natural materials may be restricted, so it is best to check local laws and transportation guidelines before returning home.

A Final Note on the Value of Amazonian Art.
The art and craft scene in the Amazon is about more than just the objects themselves; it is also about the stories they tell and the heritage they represent. Each item represents a piece of the Amazon's cultural mosaic and allows visitors to take home more than just memories. Supporting local artisans and engaging in responsible purchasing helps to preserve these age-old traditions and the vibrancy of Amazonian culture.

Traditional Cuisine and Dishes to Try

One of the most immersive ways to experience Amazonian culture is through its cuisine. The traditional dishes of the Amazon reflect the deep connection the local communities have with their environment, utilizing the abundant resources of the rainforest and river. Each dish tells a story of adaptation, resourcefulness, and cultural heritage. For travelers, trying these unique dishes provides a sensory exploration of the Amazon that is as memorable as any wildlife sighting or river excursion. Here's a guide to the traditional Amazonian cuisine and must-try dishes that offer a taste of the rainforest.

Pirarucu (Arapaima)
Pirarucu, also known as the "giant of the Amazon," is one of the world's largest freshwater fish and an Amazonian culinary staple. Its firm, white meat is low in fat and high in protein, making it suitable for a variety of preparations. Pirarucu à casaca is a baked fish dish with vegetables and herbs, while pirarucu de molho is fish cooked in a savory sauce with

traditional Amazonian seasonings. The fish's flavor is frequently compared to cod, and it is served grilled, stewed, or fried.

Try pirarucu at local markets or restaurants that focus on sustainable seafood practices. Overfishing has put pressure on pirarucu populations, so make sure the fish you eat is responsibly sourced.

Tacacá

Tacacá is a popular soup throughout the Amazon region, especially in northern Brazil. Tucupi (a yellow broth derived from cassava), jambu (a local herb known for its tongue-numbing effect), and large, fresh shrimp are used. The dish has a distinctive, tangy flavor and is served in a traditional gourd bowl known as a cuia. Tacacá is commonly consumed in the late afternoon or evening as a warming comfort food by locals.

Tip: When trying tacacá, be prepared for the numbing sensation caused by the jambu; it's a unique experience! For an authentic taste, seek out street vendors who specialize in making this dish fresh.

Maniçoba

Maniçoba is a culturally significant dish associated with the Círio de Nazaré festival in Brazil's Pará state. Maniçoba, also known as "feijoada of the Amazon," is made from cassava leaves that have been ground and boiled for several days to remove their natural toxins. The dish is then simmered with various meats, including pork and beef, to produce a rich, hearty stew. Maniçoba has a distinct, earthy flavor and is typically served with rice and farinha (toasted cassava flour).

Caution: Because maniçoba requires careful preparation to remove toxins from cassava leaves, it is best enjoyed at reputable restaurants or by experienced cooks who understand how to prepare it safely.

Pato no Tucupi (Duck In Tucupi)

Pato no tucupi is an Amazon culinary highlight that consists of duck cooked in tucupi broth, seasoned with garlic and native herbs, and served with jambu. The dish is traditionally prepared for festivals and special occasions and is a must-try for anyone looking to experience the full range of Amazonian flavors. The rich, tangy broth, combined with the tender duck meat and numbing jambu, results in a dish that is both complex and satisfying.

Suggestion: This dish is commonly found in more established restaurants serving traditional Amazonian cuisine. Look for it during the Círio de Nazaré festival or at restaurants serving regional specialties.

Moqueca de Peixe Amazonica (Amazonian Fish Stew)

While moqueca is commonly associated with coastal Brazil, the Amazon has its own twist on this fish stew. The Amazonian version frequently incorporates local fish, such as tambaqui or surubim, as well as coconut milk, cilantro, tomatoes, and regional spices. The end result is a rich, aromatic stew that exemplifies the fusion of indigenous and Portuguese influences in Amazonian cuisine.

Recommendation: Try moqueca de peixe at a local restaurant by the river for an authentic dining experience with beautiful scenery. To complete the meal, serve with rice and farofa.

Açaí na Tigela

Açaí, the small, dark purple fruit of the açaí palm, has gained global fame as a superfood. However, its roots are deeply embedded in Amazonian culture. In the Amazon, açaí is traditionally consumed in a simple, savory way, unlike the sweet bowls popular in the West. The pulp is blended into a thick, smooth texture and is commonly served with tapioca flour or fish as a staple. Its earthy, rich flavor is best enjoyed without additional sweeteners.

Tip: For an authentic experience, try freshly prepared açaí na tigela at local markets. Don't be surprised if it tastes less sweet than you're used to; the Amazonian method is more robust and true to the fruit's natural flavor.

Cocada de Castanha (Brazilian Nut Coconut Candy).

For those with a sweet tooth, cocada de castanha is a delightful Amazonian treat. This confection combines shredded coconut, Brazil nuts, and sugar to create a chewy, nutty candy that showcases two of the region's most prized ingredients. Brazil nuts, which are high in selenium, add a rich flavor to this traditional snack while also providing nutritional benefits. Cocada can usually be found at local markets or bakeries. It makes an excellent souvenir or snack during river excursions.

Farofa de banana

Farofa is a popular side dish in Brazil, and the Amazonian version frequently includes local ingredients such as bananas and nuts. Farofa de banana is made with toasted cassava flour, sliced bananas, onions, and, in some cases, Brazil nuts or other regional ingredients. The dish is both savory and slightly sweet, providing a unique flavor contrast that pairs well with main courses like grilled fish or stew.

Suggestion: Try farofa de banana as a side dish with your main course to see how the locals balance savory and sweet.

125

Advice for Dining in the Amazon

When trying Amazonian cuisine, look for local restaurants that get their ingredients from nearby producers. This promotes sustainable food practices and ensures you get the freshest flavors. Be willing to try new foods, even if the ingredients or combinations are unfamiliar. Amazonian cuisine is full of flavors reminiscent of the forest's bounty, so approach each meal with curiosity and respect for centuries-old culinary traditions.

Exploring Amazonian traditional cuisine is more than just a meal; it is a journey through the region's history, culture, and relationship with the land. Whether you're tasting savory stews, refreshing fruit drinks, or delectable sweets, these dishes offer an authentic taste of life along the river.

CHAPTER 7

ACTIVITIES AND ADVENTURES ON THE AMAZON

Canoeing, Kayaking, and River Safaris

Exploring the Amazon River by canoe, kayak, or river safari is an unforgettable way to immerse yourself in the unparalleled beauty and tranquility of this vast ecosystem. Unlike larger, motorized boats, these more intimate vessels allow you to glide quietly through hidden tributaries and narrow channels, getting up close and personal with the incredible wildlife and plant life that thrive in this unique habitat. For those seeking adventure, serenity, and a deeper connection with the rainforest, these activities provide a perspective of the Amazon that is as authentic as it is awe-inspiring.

Canoeing and Kayaking: A Personal Connection with Nature
Canoeing and kayaking provide a tranquil and intimate way to experience the Amazon's twisting waterways, where larger tour boats cannot travel. Paddling through the forest allows guests to explore the river's quieter arms and flooded woodlands, known as igapós, where each paddle stroke unveils a new surprise. These experiences frequently result in intimate encounters with animals such as pink river dolphins, sloths, capuchin monkeys, and a range of bird species including toucans and kingfishers.

For first-timers, guided canoe or kayak outings are strongly advised. Expert guides have a thorough understanding of the river's maze-like channels and are skilled at finding species that the untrained eye could miss. Their experience not only assures your safety, but also enhances your vacation by pointing out the natural behaviors and adaptations of the species you encounter. Local guides frequently give stories, legends, and insights into the rainforest's unique ecosystem, so the experience is not just physical but also educational and cultural.

Tip: The greatest times to go canoeing and kayaking are in the early morning and late afternoon. The temperature is lower, and many creatures are more active during these hours. Prepare for excessive humidity by wearing lightweight, moisture-wicking clothing with long sleeves and slacks to defend against the sun and insect bites. For further sun protection, remember to bring a wide-brimmed hat and sunglasses.

River Safaris: A broader look at the Amazon.
For those who prefer a less physically taxing approach to experience the Amazon, motorized boat safaris provide a more expansive view of the river and its tributaries. These safaris frequently involve skilled guides who lead passengers through various portions of the river, from tranquil, small inlets to the enormous main channels, where the river's strength is on full show.

River safaris are ideal for seeing larger animals like caimans, capybaras, and even jaguars relaxing on the riverbanks. The open form of the boats provides superb view for photography and animal observation. Safaris also allow you to explore rural villages or watch traditional fishing methods, which can provide cultural insights into river life.

Advice: When going on a river safari, always go with a respected operator who values sustainable and environmentally friendly operations. The adoption of quieter, more fuel-efficient engines reduces disturbance to wildlife and the environment. Bring binoculars for the best view of distant animals, and make sure your photography equipment is secured with waterproof cases or dry bags, as surprise splashes or rain showers are usual.

Canoeing in the Flooded Forests

Canoeing in the Amazon's flooded forests, or várzea, offers a one-of-a-kind magical experience. During the rainy season, the river swells, burying the forest and creating an underwater wonderland where trees appear to float on the water's surface. Paddling peacefully through these underwater forests, you'll see an ecosystem brimming with life: tree frogs clinging to branches, bright orchids blossoming above, and fish darting underneath your canoe.

Navigating these woodlands demands mindfulness and patience; the quiet waters urge you to listen to the rainforest's many noises, from the distant call of howler monkeys to the chirping of cicadas. The experience is immersive, giving guests a sense of connection that few other activities can match. Because these regions can be more difficult to travel, it is vital to be accompanied by a guide who is familiar with the forest's hidden paths and can interpret the sights and sounds.

Safety Recommendations and Cautions

- While canoeing and kayaking are quite safe, the Amazon remains a wild and unpredictable environment. Here are some important safety guidelines to keep in mind.
- Even if you are an experienced swimmer, you should always wear a life jacket. The river's currents can be powerful, and concealed hazards like as submerged branches can cause unanticipated dangers.
- Carry plenty of water and reapply sunscreen throughout your travel to stay hydrated and sun-protected.
- To avoid mosquito and other insect bites, use insect repellent, especially in the early morning and evening.
- Always follow your guide's directions, especially during wildlife interactions. While it may be tempting to kayak closer for a better view, some creatures can get frightened or hostile if they perceive a threat.
- When entering tighter channels, keep an eye out for river currents. The water may flow faster than expected, so maintaining control of your canoe or kayak is critical for safety.

Suggested itineraries and experiences

If you want to make the most of your time on the river, combine canoeing or kayaking with a guided hike or bird watching excursion. Multi-day itineraries that incorporate both land and water adventures give you a full Amazon experience, allowing you to observe the jungle from several angles. Some tours also include night canoeing excursions, where you may hear the hauntingly beautiful sounds of the forest at twilight and see nocturnal wildlife such as owls, bats, and caimans.

Final Thoughts about Responsible Exploration
Remember that the Amazon is a vulnerable ecology, thus your presence should be as minimal as possible. Choose eco-friendly tour operators and adhere to the "leave no trace" guidelines, which include taking all rubbish with you, not plucking flora or upsetting wildlife, and treating the land and water as sacred resources. Canoeing, kayaking, and river safaris are not just about excitement; they are also about developing a deeper connection with the Amazon and helping to preserve it.

Experiencing the Amazon via canoe, kayak, or river safari provides unequaled opportunities to observe the spectacular majesty and intricacy of one of the world's most incredible places. By exploring properly and respectfully, you'll learn insights that will stick with you long after the journey is over, leaving you with cherished memories and a deep appreciation for this natural wonder.

Jungle Treks and Night Excursions

Jungle treks and night excursions in the Amazon offer travelers a chance to experience the rainforest at its most raw and authentic. These activities take you beyond the riverbanks and deep into the heart of the forest, where you can witness the vibrant ecosystem up close. Every step reveals something extraordinary—whether it's a hidden waterfall, a troop of monkeys swinging through the canopy, or the symphony of insects that fills the air. Night excursions, on the other hand, showcase the rainforest's nocturnal life, an entirely different and equally fascinating side of the Amazon. For those looking to truly connect with the spirit of the jungle, these guided adventures provide a rare and intimate perspective.

The Allure of Jungle Treks
Jungle treks are suitable for visitors seeking an immersive, on-foot tour of the Amazon's dense and dynamic landscape. On these guided treks, you'll follow tiny paths flanked with towering trees, rich foliage, and tangled vines. Guides with extensive knowledge of the forest lead the journey, providing insights on the flora, wildlife, and traditional uses of plants. You may discover how indigenous cultures use tree bark for natural treatments or view medicinal plants that have been used for millennia. Wildlife

131

sightings are plentiful, with monkeys, sloths, toucans, and beautiful butterflies frequently appearing.

The cacophony of sounds is one of the most compelling aspects of a jungle trek. The rustling of leaves, distant bird calls, and the occasional splash of water provide a backdrop that is as captivating as the sights. The sensory overload of the jungle can be overwhelming at first, but as you become accustomed to its rhythm, you'll come to appreciate the balance of life that exists there.

Tips and recommendations for Jungle Treks:
- Dress correctly with lightweight, moisture-wicking apparel and durable, waterproof hiking footwear. Long sleeves and pants are required to protect against insect bites and scratches from vegetation.
- Bring a walking stick or trekking pole if you're going through uneven or slippery terrain, which is common in the rainforest.
- Carry a reusable water bottle filled with purified water to stay hydrated on your trek. Dehydration can occur quickly in a hot, humid climate.
- bag a small, waterproof day bag including essentials such as bug repellant, a rain poncho, and a compact first aid kit.
- Pay careful attention to your guide's instructions and advice. They are adept in detecting wildlife that blends in with the environment

and can warn you about concealed threats like venomous snakes or spiders.
- Avoid approaching plants or animals without the permission of your leader, as some can be toxic or aggressive when disturbed.

The Enchantment of Night Excursions

As the sun sets over the Amazon, the vegetation undergoes an incredible metamorphosis. Night expeditions provide a view into the nocturnal world, in which many jungle creatures come to life under the cover of darkness. These tours, led by experienced naturalists armed with flashlights or headlamps, take you into the darkened jungle to see a whole new range of wildlife, including owls, bats, insects, amphibians, and caimans' reflective eyes near the water's edge.

The Amazon's nighttime chorus is unforgettable, with frogs croaking, crickets chirping, and the occasional night bird screech. The sensory experience is heightened as your other senses adjust for the reduced visibility, making every rustle and distant sound more prominent. Night walks are also an opportunity to witness the glow of bioluminescent fungus, which create an unearthly effect as they illuminate sections of the forest floor.

Advice for Night Excursions:

- Equip yourself with a reliable headlamp or flashlight that has a red-light setting. Red light is less disruptive to wildlife and provides for greater night vision.
- Dress in dark or neutral colors to blend in with the surroundings and minimize startling wildlife. Lightweight, long-sleeved clothing is still recommended to protect against insects.
- Prepare for sudden weather changes. Rain can fall unexpectedly, so packing a lightweight, waterproof poncho is a good idea.
- Stay close to your guide at all times. The forest can be disorienting at night, and straying from the group raises the risk of becoming lost or encountering potentially deadly species.

- Keep noise at a minimal. Quiet movements and murmurs help to prevent scaring away nocturnal animals and allow for more accurate observations.
- Avoid utilizing flash photography. This can frighten animals, interrupt their natural behavior, and potentially impair their vision. Check with your guide if you're unsure about shooting photos.

What You Can Expect to See

During forest treks and night excursions, you may encounter a wide variety of species. During daytime walks, it's usual to see sloths lazing in the canopy, capuchin monkeys sliding gracefully through the trees, and macaws and parrots swooping overhead. You may also see leafcutter ants marching in formation or an orchid snuggled in the crook of a tree branch.

Night excursions are primarily focused on small, nocturnal animals. Tree frogs with their peculiar sounds, tarantulas emerging from their burrows, and colorful insects like enormous moths and dazzling beetles can be examined up close. One of the most amazing experiences is seeing caimans on riverbanks, their eyes reflecting a frightening red glow in the beam of a flashlight. If you're lucky, you might see a nocturnal bird or a kinkajou, a small arboreal mammal with large, curious eyes.

Responsible and Respectful Trekking

Both jungle treks and night excursions necessitate an understanding of responsible tourism practices. Stick to established trails and avoid trampling on vegetation, as even minor actions can have a long-term impact on the fragile ecosystem. Follow the "leave no trace" principle, which includes taking all trash with you and not picking plants or disturbing animal habitats. Respecting the forest and its inhabitants helps to preserve the Amazon for future generations while also promoting sustainable tourism.

Guided jungle hikes and night expeditions are some of the most remarkable and transforming activities you can do in the Amazon. With proper planning, appropriate methods, and the leadership of trained professionals, these expeditions provide unparalleled opportunity to engage with one of the most biodiverse regions on the planet. Whether admiring a sloth during the day or feeling the thrill of hearing a faraway jaguar's snarl at night, the Amazon's thick, living environment makes an indelible impact that few other experiences can rival.

Fishing for Piranhas and Other Unique Species

Fishing in the Amazon River is an experience unlike any other, offering travelers the chance to engage directly with one of the most biodiverse ecosystems in the world. Among the many fascinating fish species found in the river, the piranha stands out as both notorious and intriguing. Known for their sharp teeth and powerful jaws, piranhas have earned a reputation that often leans toward the dramatic. However, fishing for piranhas and other unique species in the Amazon is a safe and enjoyable activity when done responsibly and under the guidance of experienced local guides. Here's what to know, expect, and prepare for when embarking on this one-of-a-kind adventure.

The Experience of Fishing for Piranhas

Piranha fishing in the Amazon is as much about the excitement of the catch as it is about comprehending the intriguing behavior of these fish. Typically, fishing trips take place on lesser tributaries of the main river, where piranhas are more abundant. The procedure is straightforward but exciting: you will use a basic rod or hand line baited with raw meat or fish, which will immediately attract piranhas due to their great sense of smell.

Piranhas are surprisingly quick and aggressive feeders. When the bait touches the water, you may notice a flurry of activity as the fish gather around it. Piranha fishing is a thrilling activity that even experienced fishermen enjoy. The key is to be patient and watchful, since these fish are known to bite quickly and then retreat.

Safety Tips and Cautions

Piranhas, despite their fearsome reputation, are not the man-eating predators commonly represented in popular media. They are usually cautious and only become aggressive when provoked or during the dry season, when food is scarce. However, there are several critical safety precautions to take:

Keep your hands and feet away from the water while fishing. Piranhas are unlikely to bite unless threatened or in a feeding frenzy, so proceed with caution.

Pay attention to what your guide says. Experienced local guides understand the behavior patterns of piranhas and can ensure that your fishing trip is both safe and enjoyable. They will advise on the finest fishing places, tactics, and how to handle any fish you catch.

Handle with care. Piranhas' teeth are sharp and can readily puncture the flesh. If you catch one, let your guide or an experienced team member handle it to prevent inadvertent bites. Using gloves and tools to remove the fish from the hook is also recommended.

Beyond Piranhas: Other Unique Amazonian Fish Species.

While piranha fishing is a popular and exciting hobby, the Amazon is home to many more unique fish species worth pursuing. Here are a few.

1. Arapaima (Pirarucu)

The arapaima, also known as pirarucu, is one of the world's largest freshwater fish, reaching 10 feet in length and weighing up to 485 pounds. These fish are known for their robust, sleek bodies and remarkable ability to breathe air, and they pose a great challenge to any angler. While fishing for arapaima normally requires experienced guiding and often follows catch-and-release laws due to their protected status, the thrill of reeling in such a large fish is unparalleled.

Advice: Because of their size and strength, arapaima fishing is usually reserved for experienced anglers. Overfishing has had an influence on their populations, so always use adequate gear and respect local conservation restrictions.

2. Tambaqui.

The tambaqui is notable for its unique teeth, which mimic human molars and are used to smash nuts and fruits that fall into the water. This fish is highly appreciated for its meat, making it a favorite among locals. Because tambaqui feed mostly on seeds and plant matter, fruit-based bait is frequently used while fishing for them.

Tip: Fishing for tambaqui offers a unique view into the Amazon's interwoven ecosystem, since their eating patterns contribute to seed dispersal and rainforest health.

3. Catfish (Jau, Piraíba, and More).

The Amazon is home to several catfish species, including the massive piraíba, known as the "goliath catfish." These catfish can weigh over 400 pounds and are strong swimmers who put up a fight. Smaller species, like as the jau catfish, are also prevalent, and are distinguished by their unique whiskers and nocturnal eating patterns.

Caution: Due to the size and strength of these catfish, it is critical to utilize proper fishing equipment and collaborate closely with your guide to handle these fish safely. Large catfish can be difficult and even dangerous to reel in without correct technique.

4. Peacock Bass (Tucunaré).

For those who appreciate sport fishing, the peacock bass, or tucunaré, is a must-have. The peacock bass, known for its bright colors and aggressive temperament, is a prized capture because of the fight it puts up. Anglers frequently employ artificial lures that replicate the movement of smaller fish to attract this predator.

Recommendation: Peacock bass fishing is ideal during the dry season, when water levels are low and fish are concentrated in tiny locations. Prepare for a fast-paced and exciting adventure, as these fish are known for striking hard and fighting fiercely.

Responsible fishing practices

Fishing in the Amazon should always be done in accordance with the environment and local legislation. Many locations have catch-and-release regulations in place to assist preserve sustainable fish populations, particularly for larger species such as the arapaima. Even when fishing for piranhas or other common species, it is critical to avoid overfishing and adhere to the guidelines established by local authorities or your tour operator.

Environmental Tip: Bring reusable snack and drink containers on your fishing expedition to prevent leaving behind any waste. The Amazon environment is vulnerable, and even tiny efforts can help to preserve its natural beauty.

Engaging in Local Knowledge

Fishing expeditions provide a fantastic opportunity to learn from local fisherman and guides who have spent their entire lives navigating the river.

Their knowledge extends beyond technique; they frequently tell stories and traditions about the river, which provide dimension to the experience. Listening to their perspectives will help you appreciate the interdependence of the river's wildlife and the people who rely on it.

Fishing for piranhas and other unusual species in the Amazon is more than just a leisure sport; it's a way to connect with the river's lifeblood and learn about the delicate balance that keeps it going. Travelers who approach these activities with an attitude of respect, curiosity, and responsibility can have a wonderful trip while also contributing to the protection and enjoyment of the Amazon's vast and complex ecology.

Birdwatching and Wildlife Spotting Tours

Birdwatching and wildlife spotting tours in the Amazon are unparalleled opportunities to experience the region's biodiversity in its most vibrant and natural form. The rainforest is home to over 1,300 bird species and countless other animals, making it a prime destination for bird enthusiasts and wildlife lovers alike. These tours allow travelers to witness the diverse ecosystem up close, learning about the intricate web of life that defines this magnificent region. Here's what to expect and how to make the most of your experience.

The Magic of Birdwatching in the Amazon
The Amazon is a birder's delight, providing opportunities to witness exotic species in their natural settings. From the renowned scarlet macaw and dazzling toucan to elusive creatures like the harpy eagle, the diversity of avian life is astounding. Many birdwatching tours start around daybreak, when the birds are most active. The soft light of early morning increases visibility and highlights the vibrant colors of the rainforest's feathery denizens.

Guided birdwatching trips are vital for both novice and experienced birders, as local guides have a thorough awareness of the best places to find rare species and their cries. They frequently carry high-powered spotting scopes to help you see birds that are sitting high in the canopy or concealed among the greenery. Guides also provide vital insights into the birds' behaviors, feeding habits, and functions in the ecology, which enhances your experience.

Tip: Bring high-quality binoculars and a field guide to Amazonian bird species. Lightweight binoculars with high magnification and a broad field of view make it simpler to identify and track birds as they move quickly through dense cover.

Wildlife Spotting Tours: Beyond Birds.

While birdwatching is a big attraction, wildlife spotting expeditions offer a more comprehensive picture of the Amazon's biodiversity. These tours frequently take you down riverbanks, through flooded forests, and deep into jungle paths, where you can see a variety of species, including sloths and monkeys, caimans, and capybaras. The Amazon is famed for its diverse and often secretive fauna, so patience is essential. Even the most well-camouflaged species, such as poison dart frogs or leaf-mimic insects, can be identified by an expert guide's acute eyes.

Night wildlife spotting tours are also popular, providing an opportunity to witness nocturnal animals that are normally concealed during the day. Guides use spotlights or headlamps to accompany visitors into the nighttime jungle, pointing out species such as tarantulas, bats, and tree frogs. The forest is alive with sounds—the croaking of frogs, the buzz of insects, and the distant hoots of owls—creating an amazing sensory experience.

Recommendation: For wildlife tours, hire a guide with a solid experience in natural history and wildlife protection. Their knowledge enhances the tour and ensures that observations are conducted in a way that reduces stress for the animals and maintains their habitats.

The Best Places for Birdwatching and Wildlife Spotting

Several areas in the Amazon are known for excellent birdwatching and animal spotting opportunities:

Tambopata National Reserve (Peru): Famous for its clay licks, where hundreds of parrots and macaws congregate to feed on mineral-rich clay, Tambopata is a birdwatchers' paradise. The reserve also has a diverse wildlife population, including jaguars, giant otters, and several primate species.

Yasuni National Park (Ecuador): This park is one of the most biodiverse areas on the planet and offers excellent birdwatching opportunities with species such as the white-bellied parrot and the harpy eagle. Wildlife spotting tours frequently include journeys along the Napo River, where you can see river dolphins, caimans, and other aquatic wildlife.

Mamimaua Sustainable Development Reserve (Brazil): This reserve focuses on conservation and sustainable tourism, offering a wonderful blend of adventure and environmental understanding. It is ideal for observing pink river dolphins, caimans, and birds such as the hoatzin.

Packing Tips for Birdwatching and Wildlife Tours

Packing strategically might make your wildlife watching tour more comfortable and fruitful.

Binoculars and Camera: As previously stated, binoculars are necessary. If you enjoy taking photographs, carry a camera with a zoom lens so you can capture birds and animals from a safe distance without upsetting them.

Clothing: Wear lightweight, long-sleeved clothing in neutral or earth-toned hues to blend in and reduce bug bites. Breathable, moisture-wicking textiles are great for comfort in the humid jungle environment.

Bug repellant and Sunscreen: Mosquitoes and other insects can be annoying, so use a high-quality insect repellant before going outside. Even in the shade, the sun can be intense, so remember to use sunscreen.

Notepad and Field Guide: If you enjoy keeping track of the birds and creatures you see, a waterproof notepad and an Amazon-specific field guide are great resources.

Safety and Ethics Considerations

Ethical wildlife viewing is critical to maintaining the rainforest's fragile balance. Here are some important guidelines:

Keep Noise at a Minimum: Many animals are sensitive to noise, and loud conversations or unexpected sounds can scare them away. Maintaining a peaceful environment boosts your chances of viewing wildlife while also respecting their natural activities.

Avoid flash photography since it might disrupt and disorient animals, particularly nocturnal ones, during night tours. Always ask your guide if photography is permissible, and avoid using flash unless approved.

Stay on Designated Trails: Deviating from the trail might disrupt ecosystems and destroy the delicate environment. Trust your guides' experience; they are certified to lead groups along environmentally friendly routes.

Do not Feed or Touch Wildlife: Even if an animal appears friendly, feeding or handling it can be harmful to its health and safety. Wildlife that has been acclimated to human interaction may be more vulnerable to predators or behavioral changes.

Maximizing Your Experience.

To get the most out of your birdwatching or wildlife spotting tour, consider excursions that cater to small groups, since this provides for a more personalized experience while minimizing disturbance to the animals. Early morning trips frequently produce the most sights because many birds and animals are most active before dawn. Bring lots of water and food to stay hydrated and energized, and always follow your tour guide's directions to guarantee a safe and respectful experience.

Birdwatching and wildlife spotting in the Amazon are more than just activities; they are explorations of one of the world's most biodiverse regions. Whether you're seeing a scarlet macaw swoop overhead or spotting a capuchin monkey swinging through the trees, these experiences provide a profound connection to nature that will stay with you long after your adventure is complete.

Photography Tours and Workshops

Photography tours and workshops in the Amazon provide travelers with a unique opportunity to capture the raw beauty and vibrant biodiversity of the world's largest rainforest. The Amazon's rich landscape, teeming with wildlife, dramatic river scenes, and lush vegetation, is a paradise for photographers, from seasoned professionals to passionate hobbyists. These tours are specially designed to guide you to the best spots for breathtaking shots while helping you develop the skills needed to photograph this challenging but rewarding environment. Here's what to expect and how to make the most of a photography-focused journey through the Amazon.

Guided Tours with Expert Photographers
Photography trips in the Amazon are frequently led by skilled photographers who understand the topography, lighting conditions, and best times to capture the forest's beauty. These guides offer excellent advice on composition, camera settings, and how to anticipate wildlife behavior to capture those ideal photos. Many excursions also include local naturalist guides who help you find animals and describe their habits, ensuring you don't miss any good photo chances.

Recommendation: When booking a photography tour, look for small group sizes that allow for more customized instruction and less interruption to wildlife. The greatest trips frequently take place at lodges or eco-camps with photography-specific amenities, such as observation towers or hides for unobtrusive animal viewing.

Best Time and Places for Photography

The Amazon's light may be challenging, with strong, harsh sunshine throughout the day and deep shadows beneath the forest canopy. Early mornings and late afternoons, also known as the "golden hours," give the best circumstances for photography, with soft, warm light and increased wildlife activity. The wet season, while more difficult to travel through, provides stunning skies, lush foliage, and the spectacle of peak river levels.

The top spots for photography in the Amazon include:

Tambopata National Reserve (Peru): Great for bird photography, especially near the clay licks where hundreds of parrots and macaws gather.

Mamirauá Sustainable Development Reserve (Brazil): Provides rare opportunity to photograph pink river dolphins, caimans, and picturesque flooded woodlands.

Yasuni National Park (Ecuador): This park is known for its great biodiversity and offers numerous opportunities to shoot unusual wildlife and beautiful plant life.

Packing the Right Gear

The appropriate equipment may make or break your shooting experience on Amazon. The following items are essential.

Camera with a Zoom Lens: A DSLR or mirrorless camera with a versatile zoom lens (e.g., 70-300mm or 100-400mm) is ideal for capturing wildlife at a distance. A wide-angle lens (e.g., 16-35mm) is useful for capturing broad panoramas and forest scenes when shooting landscapes.

Waterproof Protection: The Amazon's humidity and sudden rain showers can be harsh on your equipment. Waterproof camera bags, lens covers, and silica gel packets can all help protect your equipment from dampness.

Tripod or Monopod: These are particularly useful for long exposure shots or when photographing birds in low light. A lightweight, durable tripod or monopod that can be adjusted for uneven terrain is ideal.

Spare Batteries and Memory Cards: Wildlife photography can quickly deplete batteries, particularly when using autofocus and picture stabilization features. Bring extra batteries and memory cards to ensure you don't miss any important moments.

Tips for Taking Stunning Photos

1. Mastering the Light: The dappled sunlight flowing through the canopy, along with rapid weather changes, makes lighting unpredictable. Spot metering and manual exposure adjustments can help you balance highlights and shadows in your photos. Golden hour is ideal for early morning and late afternoon photography because it produces softer light that highlights details and adds warmth to your images.

2. Silent Shooting and Patience: The Amazon's fauna is frequently elusive and easily disturbed by noise. To avoid scaring away possible subjects, use your camera's silent photography mode. Patience is essential; it may be necessary to wait silently for several minutes or more to see a bird or animal emerge from the trees.

3. Capture Motion and Stillness: Include both motion and still images in your portfolio. Slow shutter speeds can be used to blur waterfalls or catch the movement of fish swimming in shallow waterways, whilst faster shutter speeds can freeze birds in flight or monkeys leaping between branches.

4. Concentrate on Details and the Big Picture: Don't limit yourself to larger creatures or expansive landscapes. Close-ups of intricate spider webs, dew on leaves, and the vibrant hues of butterflies give dimension to your picture collection while also telling a more complete tale about the Amazon ecology.

Workshops & Hands-on Training

Workshops offer a more controlled learning environment for photographers wishing to enhance their talents. These courses, often given by expert photographers, include lectures on camera settings, composition, and post-processing techniques specific to rainforest photography. Workshops may involve guided walks in which instructors provide on-the-spot assistance to help you frame and capture the best images of the various subjects you encounter.

Advice: Before booking a workshop, make sure the instructor has prior experience with jungle or animal photography. This expertise guarantees that they understand the Amazon's particular obstacles, such as changing light conditions and the necessity to work swiftly before animals passes out of sight.

Remaining Ethical and Respectful

Photography in the Amazon must be done ethically to protect both wildlife and local communities. Avoid using flash when photographing animals, as it might confuse and distress them, especially nocturnal species. Respect the privacy and wishes of the locals, and always obtain permission before photographing them. Many communities appreciate their traditions and may have special rules on how and when photography is permitted.

Recommendation: When photographing individuals or engaging in cultural events, aim to capture the essence of the moment rather than staging images. This method demonstrates respect and frequently produces more honest, meaningful photos.

Caution: Be cautious of your surroundings at all times, especially when looking through your camera's viewfinder. The jungle may be unpredictable, with sudden changes in weather, rough terrain, and surprise wildlife sightings. Always prioritize safety and pay attention to your guide's directions.

Photography excursions and courses in the Amazon are an excellent way to expand your knowledge of the rainforest while polishing your skills behind the camera. Whether you're photographing the vibrant plumage of a macaw, the peaceful serenity of the river at sunrise, or the fine intricacies of the forest floor, these experiences produce enduring memories and photos that reflect the wonder of one of the world's most unique places.

CHAPTER 8

SUSTAINABLE AND RESPONSIBLE TOURISM

Minimizing Your Environmental Impact

Traveling to the Amazon is a rare and enriching experience, but it comes with a responsibility to protect this delicate and vital ecosystem. The Amazon rainforest is not only one of the most biodiverse places on Earth but also plays a critical role in regulating the global climate and supporting indigenous communities. Sustainable and responsible tourism can ensure that your visit contributes to the protection and preservation of this incredible region. Here are essential practices and guidelines for minimizing your environmental impact while enjoying the Amazon.

1. Choose Eco-Friendly Tour Operators

One of the most effective methods to reduce your environmental impact is to book a tour with a focus on sustainability. Look for operators who use environmentally responsible practices such as fuel-efficient boats, limit group sizes, and collaborate with local communities to promote conservation efforts. Eco-lodges recognized by respected organizations and committed to sustainable methods, such as the use of renewable energy, waste management systems, and water conservation measures, are ideal choices.

Ask your tour operator about their environmental practices and any ties they have with local conservation groups. Supporting operators who hire local guides and staff helps to redirect resources back into the community and fosters a sense of ownership in the preservation of their property.

2. Travel lightly and avoid single-use plastics.

Packing light not only saves gasoline while traveling, but it also makes it easier to move around sustainably in the rainforest. Avoid bringing products that cause trash, such as single-use plastics. Instead, use reusable products such as water bottles, cloth shopping bags, and silicone storage containers. Many eco-lodges and tour companies have filtered water stations, so pack a high-quality reusable bottle to replenish throughout your journey.

Caution: material disposal is difficult in rural regions, so any non-biodegradable material you generate should be packed out and properly disposed of when you return to more urban areas.

3. Stick to the designated paths and guidelines.
The Amazon is a highly sensitive environment, and even modest perturbations can have long-term consequences. Always stay on approved paths and obey the directions of your tour leader or guide. Wandering off-trail can harm plants, disrupt wildlife habitats, and increase the likelihood of encountering potentially deadly creatures. Guides are trained to conduct people in methods that minimize environmental impact while increasing opportunities to see wildlife and unusual vegetation.

Advice: Follow any rules established by local communities or reserves about off-limit zones. These limits are frequently put in place to safeguard both visitors and the environment.

4. Practice responsible wildlife viewing.
The Amazon's fauna is one of its most attractive features, however contact with animals must be managed appropriately. Avoid behaviors that can stress or injure wildlife, such as utilizing flash photography or creating loud sounds. Never feed animals, as this can cause reliance, interrupt natural feeding behaviors, and put them in danger if they approach humans in the future. Maintain a safe distance at all times to prevent any disruption to their natural behavior.

Tip: If you want to shoot wildlife, carry equipment that allows you to zoom in from a distance rather than approaching them too closely. Follow ethical photography methods to guarantee that your presence does not harm the animals.

5. Support local conservation efforts.

Many conservation organizations operate in the Amazon, focused on reforestation, wildlife protection, and indigenous community development. Consider engaging in or donating to these projects during your visit. Some tour operators collaborate with conservation groups to offer eco-volunteering programs in which tourists can give their time and expertise to ongoing projects.

Recommendation: Before donating or participating in a program, conduct research to confirm that the group is credible and that the cash or efforts are being used properly.

6. Reduce water and energy usage.

Water and energy conservation are crucial in the Amazon, particularly in remote lodges with limited supplies. Simple steps, such as turning off lights, fans, and air conditioning while not in use, can have a substantial impact. Limit your shower time and be aware of water usage, as many resorts rely on rainwater or river water for supply.

Caution: Be aware of the toiletries you use. Choose biodegradable soaps, shampoos, and conditioners to avoid contaminating the rivers. The Amazon's rivers and streams support a diverse range of aquatic species, and even trace amounts of chemical contaminants can have negative consequences.

7. Leave No Trace.

When visiting the Amazon, it is critical to practice "Leave No Trace" principles. This includes bringing all rubbish, including biodegradable items such as fruit peels or tissues, with you when you depart. Even seemingly harmless products might have a negative impact on the surrounding ecosystem. Avoid plucking plants, gathering rocks, or disrupting animal habitats. Every modest activity helps to ensure the overall survival of this delicate environment.

Final Tip: Before your travel, become acquainted with eco-friendly behaviors and commit to practicing them during your stay. By making these efforts, you will help to preserve the Amazon's natural beauty and ensure that future generations can enjoy it as you have.

When visiting the Amazon, you can reduce your environmental effect by following these tips and adopting sustainable habits. Responsible tourism not only improves your experience, but it also helps to preserve one of the world's most remarkable natural beauties.

Supporting Local Communities and Eco-Friendly Initiatives

Supporting local communities and eco-friendly initiatives while visiting the Amazon is integral to fostering sustainable tourism that benefits both the environment and the people who call the rainforest home. The Amazon region is rich not only in biodiversity but also in cultural heritage, and engaging in responsible tourism practices helps ensure that both are preserved for future generations. Here's how travelers can contribute meaningfully and make their visits more impactful.

1. Choose Locally Owned Accommodations and Tours
One of the simplest ways to help local communities is to stay in lodges or eco-camps run by locals. These lodgings frequently employ community residents, offer training opportunities, and keep earnings in the local economy. Choosing locally owned tour operators also assures that your trip is led by those who are most knowledgeable about the area, its history, and cultural value. These guides deliver vital knowledge and insights that enrich your adventure by providing a greater understanding of the Amazon's flora, animals, and cultures.

Recommendation: Look for lodges that stress sustainability and community participation. Look for hotels that employ local resources in their construction, fund forestry projects, or donate a portion of their profits to community development programs.

2. Buy locally made products.
When visiting Amazonian villages and markets, look for handmade things such as crafts, textiles, jewelry, and pottery. Purchasing these items directly benefits artists and their families by providing a vital source of income. Furthermore, many of these crafts are produced utilizing ancient

methods passed down through generations, thereby conserving the region's cultural legacy. Buying locally not only gives you a meaningful souvenir, but it also helps to preserve craft knowledge.

Caution: Be wary of the products you buy. Avoid products containing endangered animal parts, unsustainable wood, or other components that may contribute to deforestation or wildlife harm. Ethical purchase benefits both the environment and humans.

3. Participate in community-based experiences.

Participating in activities or workshops organized by local communities is an effective method to demonstrate support and obtain a better understanding of Amazonian culture. These experiences may include guided forest hikes with indigenous tribes, cooking workshops including traditional dishes, or storytelling sessions that bring the region's culture to life. Participation in such events directly benefits community residents and promotes cultural exchange, allowing visitors and locals to share and learn from one another.

Tip: Ask your guide or tour operator for advice on community-led, ethically managed experiences. Ensure that every activity in which you participate respects the community's cultural norms and traditions while also contributing positively to their well-being.

4. Support environmentally friendly projects and initiatives.

The Amazon is home to a number of environmentally friendly activities focused at conservation, replanting, and sustainable resource management. Some lodges and tour companies collaborate with these programs, letting tourists to participate by participating or donating. For example, you may participate in a tree-planting activity, support wildlife monitoring projects, or donate to programs that promote sustainable farming methods in local communities. These efforts are critical to protecting the Amazon's fragile ecosystems and instilling a feeling of responsibility in local communities.

Recommendation: If you decide to donate to conservation efforts, study the organization to ensure that it works transparently and effectively. Partnering with established programs ensures that your contribution has a meaningful impact.

5. Be respectful and culturally aware.

Respectful interaction with local communities is essential for providing effective help. This includes knowing and respecting cultural traditions, obtaining permission before shooting images, and remaining open-minded and attentive while learning about their way of life. Many communities welcome visitors who are genuinely interested in their traditions and rituals, but they may be wary or guarded around those who look contemptuous or invasive.

Advice: As a sign of respect, learn a few basic phrases in the local language or dialect. Simple phrases like "thank you" or "hello" can go a long way toward demonstrating that you respect their culture.

6. Prioritize education and awareness.

Understanding the issues that Amazonian communities confront enables travelers to become more effective advocates for their well-being. Issues like as deforestation, illegal mining, and climate change endanger both the environment and those who rely on it. Learning about these difficulties and sharing your knowledge when you return home will help raise awareness and urge others to support conservation and responsible tourism.

Suggestion: Attend presentations or workshops led by local environmental and community leaders to acquire personal knowledge of the efforts to safeguard the Amazon. Use what you've learned to educate others and lobby for policies that promote sustainable tourism and conservation activities.

7. Partner with social enterprises.

Social companies in the Amazon frequently help to bridge the gap between conservation initiatives and local development. These groups help communities by supporting sustainable practices like organic farming, ecotourism, and the production of renewable resources. Collaborating with or purchasing products from these companies directly supports their purpose and promotes a development strategy that emphasizes people and the environment.

Caution: Be aware of companies who claim to be environmentally friendly but lack certifications and transparency. Trustworthy firms will share transparent information on how their operations help local communities and ecosystems.

Supporting local communities and eco-friendly activities in the Amazon improves your trip experience while also benefiting the region's long-term well-being. By choosing to participate deliberately and ethically, you actively contribute to the preservation of this incomparable destination's unique culture and ecology.

How to Be a Respectful Visitor to Indigenous Lands

Visiting indigenous lands in the Amazon is an extraordinary privilege that offers a glimpse into cultures that have lived in harmony with the rainforest for centuries. These communities hold profound knowledge of the ecosystem and traditions that are deeply rooted in their identity. As a visitor, it's essential to approach your experience with respect, mindfulness, and an open heart. Here's how to ensure that your visit is respectful and positive for both you and the communities you encounter.

1. Learn About the Community Before You Go
Taking the time to learn about the indigenous group's culture, traditions, and customs shows respect and genuine interest in their way of life. Researching the community's history, beliefs, and issues allows you to approach your visit with greater sensitivity and awareness. It can also help you prepare for any cultural traditions or protocols that you may encounter during your visit, such as greetings, clothing restrictions, or ceremonies.

Tip: To learn more about the place you're visiting, consult credible sources like books, documentaries, or information offered by your tour operator. Your guide can also provide useful context before you arrive.

2. Follow Cultural Etiquette.
Every indigenous society follows its unique set of customs and social standards. Being cognizant of these practices is essential for demonstrating

respect. For example, in some Amazonian tribes, it may be inappropriate to touch particular artifacts or access specific regions without permission. Always wait for guidance before engaging in any rituals or ceremonies, and follow any instructions given by your hosts or guide.

When visiting, dress modestly in lightweight, long-sleeved clothing and long pants to demonstrate respect and protect oneself from insects. Neutral or earth-toned hues are frequently favored since they fit in better with the natural environment and indicate that you are aware of your presence in the neighborhood.

3. Get permission before taking photos.
Photographs can preserve valuable memories, but in many indigenous groups, photography bears a deeper meaning. Always seek permission before photographing people, residences, or sacred locations. Some communities may hold spiritual beliefs about photography or simply appreciate their privacy. If a community or person denies your photo request, respect their wishes without putting them under any pressure.

Caution: Avoid utilizing flash photography because it can be distracting and obtrusive, especially during religious or sensitive events.

4. Support local artisans and businesses.
Purchasing locally manufactured crafts, fabrics, or foods is one way to express gratitude and support to the community. Purchasing directly from craftsmen supports their livelihoods and preserves traditional crafts. Whether it's handcrafted jewelry, woven baskets, or herbal cures, these objects frequently come with stories and meanings that help you better appreciate the culture.

Recommendation: Avoid bargaining over pricing when purchasing from local craftspeople. The price of handcrafted objects frequently reflects the time, effort, and talent necessary to make them. Paying a fair price recognizes the worth of their labor and adds to their financial well-being.

5. Engage in meaningful interactions.
Engage with community members in a courteous and sincere manner. Listening is a significant learning tool, so express real interest in their

experiences, customs, and viewpoints. If you have any questions, ask them nicely and be receptive to anything they are ready to offer. Establishing a connection based on mutual respect and curiosity can result in meaningful conversations that go beyond the conventional tourist experience.

Tip: Learning a few basic words or phrases in the local language is a good approach to demonstrate your interest in their culture. Simple pleasantries or comments such as "thank you" can go a long way toward building rapport and demonstrating that you value their way of life.

6. Respect sacred spaces and practices.
Many indigenous societies consider certain sites or artifacts sacred. Whether it's a ceremonial location, a specific tree, or a body of water, these areas are frequently off-limits or require special permission to enter. Follow your guide's recommendations concerning where you can and cannot go, and always inquire before participating in or observing rituals. Entering a sacred area without permission can be considered extremely rude and disturbing.

Advice: If requested to attend or participate in a ceremony, keep a modest and respectful manner. Avoid taking photos unless officially permitted, and do not interrupt or ask questions during the rite.

7. Avoid making assumptions or passing judgment.
It's critical to go into your vacation with an open mind and avoid making assumptions based on your own cultural expectations. Life in an indigenous society may differ from what you are used to, but it does not make it any less valid or sophisticated. Many of these groups have altered their lifestyles to fit the rainforest environment, exemplifying the balance that contemporary life frequently lacks. Be prepared to learn and question your assumptions.

Caution: Do not compare their way of life to your own or provide unwanted advise. Comments that are well-intentioned may come across as dismissive or critical. Remember that you are a guest in their home, and their conventions deserve your complete respect.

8. Leave No Trace.

When visiting Indigenous territories, follow the "leave no trace" philosophy. This includes taking any rubbish with you when you leave and avoiding harming plants or animals. The preservation of the ecosystem is critical not just for the community's way of life, but also for the overall health of the rainforest.

Recommendation: Use reusable products like water bottles and eco-friendly toiletries to minimize your effect. Be cautious of your consumption and avoid bringing goods that could cause waste or pollution.

Visiting indigenous territories in the Amazon is a privilege that with the responsibility of being a courteous visitor. Following these principles will ensure that your presence has a beneficial impact on the community and allows you to obtain a deeper, more authentic understanding of their culture. This conscious approach enhances your trip experience while also protecting the traditions and ecosystem of these unique villages for future generations.

Resources for Learning More About Amazonian Conservation

Understanding and supporting Amazonian conservation goes beyond the boundaries of travel. Whether you're planning a visit, reflecting on a recent journey, or simply interested in contributing to the preservation of this unique ecosystem, numerous resources can deepen your knowledge and involvement. From organizations and books to documentaries and educational courses, here are some of the best resources for learning more about Amazonian conservation and how you can help protect this vital region.

1. Conservation Organizations
There are numerous reputable organizations working to protect the Amazon rainforest and support its indigenous communities. These organizations work tirelessly to combat deforestation, illegal mining, and biodiversity loss while also advocating for indigenous people's rights.

Amazon Conservation Association (ACA): The ACA is dedicated to protecting Amazon biodiversity and promoting sustainable development through a variety of projects, including research stations and reforestation efforts.

Rainforest Alliance: Known for its global initiatives, the Rainforest Alliance collaborates directly with communities and businesses to develop sustainable livelihoods that protect forests and their biodiversity.

WWF (World Wildlife Fund) Amazon Program: The WWF's Amazon Program encompasses a wide range of conservation efforts, including combating deforestation and promoting local and indigenous community rights.

Amazon Watch: This organization partners with indigenous groups to advocate for their rights and promote rainforest protection. Their work includes campaigns against destructive industries and policy advocacy.

Tip: If you want to gain hands-on experience in conservation, consider donating to these organizations or looking into volunteer opportunities.

2. Documentaries and films.
Visual storytelling is a powerful tool for understanding the Amazon's complexity and beauty. Documentaries and films can shed light on the challenges facing the rainforest and the efforts being made to protect it.

"River of Gold": This documentary examines the devastation caused by illegal gold mining in the Amazon, as well as the impact on indigenous communities and biodiversity.

"Amazonia: The Last Forest": This film examines the relationship between the rainforest and its indigenous protectors, as well as how traditional knowledge and practices contribute to conservation efforts.

"Jungle Mystery: Lost Kingdoms of the Amazon": This series delves into the history, archaeology, and current threats to the Amazon, offering a multifaceted perspective on its importance.

"Planet Earth II - Jungles": While not entirely focused on the Amazon, this episode of the acclaimed series offers breathtaking visuals and fascinating insights into the rainforest's ecosystem.

3. Books & Literature
Books provide a thorough exploration of the Amazon's history, culture, biodiversity, and conservation efforts. Whether you prefer nonfiction or narratives, there is something for every reader.

"The Unconquered: In Search of the Amazon's Last Uncontacted Tribes" by Scott Wallace. This book follows the journey of a team assigned to protect one of the Amazon's last uncontacted tribes, providing insight into indigenous rights and conservation challenges.

"One River" by Wade Davis: A look at the Amazon's rich history and the life of Richard Evans Schultes, the father of modern ethnobotany, who studied how indigenous people use plants for medicine and rituals.

"State of Wonder" by Ann Patchett While fiction, this novel immerses readers in the beauty and mystery of the Amazon rainforest while also raising thought-provoking questions about pharmaceutical exploration and its impact on indigenous communities.

"Tree of Rivers: The Story of the Amazon" by John Hemming. A detailed history of the Amazon, from its early exploration to current conservation challenges.

4. Educational Courses and Workshops

For those who prefer a more structured learning approach, educational courses and workshops can provide detailed and comprehensive information about Amazonian conservation.

Conservation Biology Courses: Several universities and conservation organizations provide online courses on tropical ecology, conservation strategies, and sustainable development. Look into platforms like Coursera, EdX, and FutureLearn for programs that include Amazon-specific content.

Rainforest Alliance Workshops: The Rainforest Alliance hosts webinars and workshops on a regular basis to provide more information about their conservation efforts, sustainable practices, and how the public can help.

Amazon Research Expeditions: Some organizations and eco-lodges provide immersive workshops and expeditions for visitors who want to learn about conservation practices firsthand. These include biologist-led tours, sustainable living workshops, and volunteer research programs.

5. Podcasts & Audio Resources

Podcasts provide a flexible way to stay informed and expand your knowledge of Amazonian conservation and related topics.

"The Wild" by Christopher Morgan: This podcast looks at different wild places and conservation efforts around the world. Episodes about the Amazon feature engaging stories and interviews with conservationists and local experts.

"The Amazon Conservation Podcast": This podcast focuses on conservation efforts in the Amazon, discussing various challenges, success stories, and the work of various organizations and communities.

"Voices of the Rainforest" is an audio documentary that takes listeners on a soundscape journey through the rainforest, blending nature sounds with indigenous communities' music and rituals to create a one-of-a-kind listening experience.

6. Sustainable Travel Guides

Sustainable travel guides provide advice on how to visit the Amazon responsibly and promote environmentally friendly practices while there.

"The Responsible Traveler's Guide to the Amazon": While this is not a specific publication, look for articles and guides on sustainable tourism from established travel writers and conservation organizations. These guides frequently provide practical advice on how to select ethical tour operators, interact respectfully with local communities, and reduce environmental impact.

Advice: Keep up with current conservation news while reading a book, watching a documentary, or taking an online course. Follow Amazon-specific organizations and conservationists on social media for real-time updates and insights.

Exploring these resources will give you a better understanding of the Amazon's importance, the challenges it faces, and the efforts being made to protect it. Your informed awareness can help to increase conservation efforts and empower you to make more responsible decisions as a traveler and advocate for this unique and important region.

What to Bring Back Home from the Amazon Rainforest

When visiting the Amazon Rainforest, the memories and experiences you gain are the most valuable souvenirs. However, bringing home items that capture the essence of the region can make your journey even more memorable and help support local communities. To ensure that your purchases are sustainable and respectful of the environment, here are some recommended items to consider bringing back, along with tips on how to choose responsibly.

1. Handcrafted Art and Jewelry
The Amazon is home to incredible artisans who craft beautiful, one-of-a-kind pieces out of natural materials. Handmade necklaces, bracelets, and earrings made from seeds, beads, and sustainably sourced fibers are not only one-of-a-kind, but also deeply rooted in local traditions. Each piece often tells a story and captures the natural beauty of the rainforest.

Recommendation: Look for products made from non-endangered seeds and natural fibers, such as huayruro seeds, which are known for their distinct red and black colors and are thought to bring good luck. Supporting local artisans directly helps to preserve their craft and provides economic benefits to their families and communities.

Caution: Avoid purchasing items containing feathers, animal parts, or materials derived from protected or endangered species. Always inquire about the origin of the materials used to ensure that your purchase promotes ethical and sustainable practices.

2. Traditional textiles and woven baskets.
Textiles and woven items are another great way to bring a bit of the Amazon home. Handwoven baskets, mats, and textiles are frequently made with traditional techniques passed down through generations. They can be both decorative and functional, bringing a touch of Amazonian culture into your home.

Tip: Look for textiles with traditional patterns and designs that reflect the cultural identity of individual indigenous groups. Purchasing directly from artisans at local markets ensures that your money supports the community and helps to preserve traditional weaving practices.

3. Natural Beauty and Wellness Products.

163

The Amazon is famous for its diverse collection of plants with medicinal and wellness properties. Many local markets sell natural beauty products such as soaps, oils, and balms made with Amazonian ingredients like copaiba oil, buriti oil, and Brazil nut oil. These products are known for their moisturizing and healing properties, and they allow you to reap the benefits of the rainforest long after your visit.

Check that these products are sustainably sourced and free of harmful additives. Choose handmade items that are packaged in eco-friendly materials to reduce your environmental impact.

4. Artisan Foods and Spices

Bringing home unique flavors from the Amazon is a tasty way to commemorate your trip. Spices like cumaru (also known as tonka bean), exotic fruit jams, and sustainably harvested Brazil nuts are popular options. These items make excellent gifts and allow you to share a taste of Amazon with friends and family.

Recommendation: Make sure that any food products you bring into your home country are legally permitted, as some may be subject to import restrictions. In addition, select products that are sustainably harvested and support local farmers.

5. Book and Educational Materials

Books written by local authors or about Amazonian culture, history, and conservation make great souvenirs. These materials allow you to learn about the region even after you leave, while also supporting local writers and publishers.

Visit local bookstores or community centers to find authentic literature about the stories, myths, and daily lives of Amazonian communities. Purchasing these materials contributes to education and the preservation of local heritage.

6. Eco-friendly Handicrafts

Sustainable crafts made from bamboo, coconut shells, and recycled materials demonstrate the creativity and resourcefulness of local artisans.

These items could include utensils, decorative items, or eco-friendly home goods that add a distinct Amazonian flair to your living space.

Advice: Inquire with the seller about the materials used in these products, and select items that do not contribute to deforestation or harm wildlife. Supporting crafts made from recycled and sustainable materials encourages environmentally friendly practices in the region.

7. Musical Instruments

The Amazon is home to a diverse range of indigenous musical instruments, including hand-carved flutes, gourd maracas, and percussion. These items not only serve as beautiful reminders of your journey, but also allow you to participate in the region's musical traditions.

Caution: Ensure that any instruments you purchase are made from sustainable materials and do not contain animal parts or endangered woods. Always confirm with the seller that the item was made ethically.

8. Pottery & Ceramics

Amazonian artisans frequently use intricate designs and patterns in their clay pots, vases, and other ceramics to reflect the region's natural and cultural influences. These items can be used as functional pieces or decorative art in your home, reminding you of the rich craftsmanship of Amazon.

Recommendation: When purchasing pottery, inquire about the techniques and materials used to ensure that it was made in a sustainable and traditional manner. Supporting artisans who make their products by hand helps to preserve these important cultural practices.

What Not to Bring Home

While it is tempting to bring back natural souvenirs like shells, rocks, or plants, these items should not be taken from the rainforest. Removing elements from their natural habitat can upset the local ecosystem and contribute to environmental degradation. Furthermore, certain plant and animal products may be illegal to export or import, resulting in fines or legal issues.

Advice: Buy from local markets, artisans, and reputable vendors to ensure that your purchases benefit the region's economy and biodiversity.

By carefully selecting what to bring home from the Amazon, you can create a meaningful memento of your trip that benefits local communities, promotes sustainable practices, and preserves the region's unparalleled beauty and cultural heritage.

CHAPTER 9

HEALTH AND SAFETY ESSENTIALS FOR THE AMAZON RIVER

Navigating Health Risks and Insect Precautions

Traveling to the Amazon River can be the adventure of a lifetime, but it also comes with unique health and safety challenges. From the region's tropical climate and abundant wildlife to the remote locations and potential health risks, proper preparation and vigilance are essential to ensuring a safe and enjoyable journey. Here's what you need to know to stay healthy and safe while exploring this incredible region.

1. Vaccinations and Preventative Medicine

Before traveling to the Amazon, you should consult with a travel health specialist or your primary care physician at least 4-6 weeks before your trip. The following vaccinations and precautions are commonly recommended for travelers:

Yellow Fever Vaccine: Because the Amazon region is endemic for yellow fever, this vaccine is essential. Many countries also require proof of vaccination when you return.

Typhoid and Hepatitis A Vaccines: Because both diseases can be transmitted through contaminated food or water, these vaccines are strongly recommended.

Malaria Prophylaxis: Because malaria is prevalent in many parts of the Amazon, consult your doctor about taking antimalarial medication before and during your visit. Remember that no preventive treatment is completely effective, so mosquito control measures are also required.

Rabies Vaccine: If you plan to spend a significant amount of time outside or in remote areas with limited medical facilities, consider getting the rabies vaccine.

Advice: Keep a record of your vaccinations and any medications you bring with you, and make a digital backup.

2. Insect Protection.
In the Amazon, insects, particularly mosquitos, can be a major nuisance and health risk. These insects can transmit diseases such as malaria, dengue fever, Zika virus, and yellow fever. Protecting yourself from insect bites is critical.

Use Insect Repellent: For long-term protection, choose a repellent containing DEET, picaridin, or lemon eucalyptus oil. Apply generously to exposed skin and clothing.

Wear Appropriate Clothing: Long-sleeved shirts, long pants, and socks are necessary to reduce exposed skin. Light-colored clothing is recommended because it is less appealing to mosquitos.

Mosquito Nets: When sleeping in lodges or on boats, ensure that mosquito nets are in place, particularly in more basic accommodations. If possible, use treated nets for added protection.

Caution: Reapply insect repellent after sweating or swimming to keep it effective.

3. Staying hydrated and avoiding waterborne illnesses
The Amazon's humid climate can cause dehydration if you don't drink enough water. Always carry a reusable water bottle and fill it with purified or filtered water. Tap water in the Amazon is generally unsafe for drinking, so it is critical to use treated water.

Drink Purified Water: If bottled or treated water is unavailable, use water purification tablets or a portable water filter.

Avoid Ice and Raw Foods: Ice cubes are frequently made with tap water, so avoid them unless you know they were made with purified water. To reduce the risk of waterborne illnesses, avoid eating raw foods such as salads and unpeeled fruit.

Recommendation: Bring oral rehydration salts to prevent dehydration, especially if you'll be doing physically demanding activities like hiking or canoeing.

4. Food Safety.
Eating local cuisine is part of the experience; however, taking precautions can help you avoid foodborne illnesses.

Choose Cooked Foods: Select dishes that are thoroughly cooked and served hot. Avoid street food unless it comes from a reliable source that practices good hygiene.

Wash and Peel Fruits: To reduce the risk of contamination, stick with fruits that you can peel yourself, such as bananas and oranges.

Avoid Dairy Products: Unless they have been pasteurized, dairy products can pose a risk in some areas.

Tip: Keep a small bottle of hand sanitizer with at least 60% alcohol on hand in case soap and water are not available.

5. First Aid Essentials
Packing a comprehensive first aid kit is essential because medical facilities can be scarce and difficult to reach in remote areas. Your kit should contain:

Basic Supplies: Adhesive bandages, sterile gauze, adhesive tape, and antiseptic wipes.

Medications include pain relievers, antihistamines for allergic reactions, antidiarrheal tablets, motion sickness medication, and any personal prescriptions.

Insect Bite Treatment: Hydrocortisone cream and antihistamine tablets can help with itching and swelling from insect bites.

Antibiotics: Consider bringing a general antibiotic prescribed by your doctor to treat infections that may occur in remote areas.

Advice: To avoid customs issues, ensure that all medications are clearly labeled and packed in their original containers.

6. How to safely navigate wildlife encounters.

The Amazon is home to a diverse range of wildlife, some of which are potentially dangerous. While wildlife encounters rarely pose a significant threat, it is important to take precautions.

Stay alert and follow your guide's instructions. Guided tours are the safest way to explore the Amazon because experienced guides understand how to avoid dangerous situations and keep you informed about animal behavior.

Avoid touching animals: Even seemingly harmless creatures can carry diseases or react unexpectedly to human contact. This rule applies to both wild and domesticated animals.

Maintain Food Security: Store food securely and avoid leaving scraps behind, as they can attract unwanted visitors such as monkeys or more dangerous animals such as jaguars and caimans.

Caution: Do not approach or feed any wildlife, as this can endanger both yourself and the animals.

7. Sun and Heat Protection.

The tropical sun can be intense, so proper protection is required:

Wear Sunscreen: Use a broad-spectrum sunscreen with an SPF of at least 30 and reapply every two hours, or more frequently if you sweat or swim.

Wear a hat and sunglasses: A wide-brimmed hat and polarized sunglasses will shield your face and eyes from the sun's glare.

Take Breaks in the Shade: Rest frequently, especially if you're exercising during the hottest hours of the day.

Final Tip: Pay attention to how you feel throughout your journey. If you experience dizziness, headaches, or nausea, take it as a cue to rest, hydrate, and cool down.

By adhering to these health and safety guidelines, you can ensure that your Amazon River adventure is both safe and enjoyable, allowing you to fully appreciate the wonders of this unique and majestic ecosystem.

First Aid and Emergency Protocols

When venturing into the Amazon, where medical facilities can be sparse and emergency assistance may take time to arrive, having a well-thought-out first aid plan and understanding emergency protocols is essential. Preparing for potential health issues and knowing how to respond effectively in case of an emergency will enhance your safety and peace of mind during your journey. Here's a comprehensive guide on first aid essentials and what to do if you face an emergency in the Amazon.

1. Packing a Comprehensive First Aid Kit
A well-stocked first aid kit is crucial when traveling in remote areas like the Amazon. Make sure your kit includes:

- Basic supplies include adhesive bandages, sterile gauze, adhesive tape, and antiseptic wipes for minor cuts and abrasions.
- Over-the-counter pain relievers and anti-inflammatory medications, such as ibuprofen or acetaminophen, can be used to treat aches, pains, and fevers.

- Antihistamines are used to treat allergic reactions, such as bites, stings, and unexpected plant allergies.
- Antiseptic Cream or Spray: Used to disinfect and prevent infection in cuts or insect bites.
- Insect Bite Relief: Use hydrocortisone cream or other anti-itch solutions to treat insect bites or mild rashes.
- Anti-Diarrheal and Rehydration Solutions: These are essential for preventing dehydration and dealing with stomach issues.
- Prescription medications include any personal prescriptions that are clearly labeled, as well as extra doses in case of travel delays.
- Antibiotics: Speak with your doctor about carrying a broad-spectrum antibiotic to treat bacterial infections.
- Sterile tweezers and scissors are useful for removing splinters and cutting bandages.
- Burn Relief Gel or Cream: Treats minor burns and sunburns.
- Thermometer: A compact digital thermometer can help monitor fevers.

Tip: To ensure compliance with customs regulations and proper labeling, keep all medications in their original packaging.

2. Emergency Contact and Communication Devices

Given the remote nature of the Amazon, it's critical to have a reliable way to communicate in case of an emergency:

Emergency Numbers and Contacts: Before you travel, make sure you have the emergency contact information for the local authorities, nearest medical facilities, and your country's embassy or consulate.

Satellite Phone or Radio: In areas where cellular service is unavailable, a satellite phone or emergency radio can be used to contact emergency services or your tour operator.

GPS Device: A handheld GPS device can assist rescuers in determining your exact location, which is critical if you need to report an emergency.

If you're traveling with a group or a guide, make an emergency communication plan before you begin your adventure. Ensure that everyone understands the procedure for contacting help and reporting your location.

3. Addressing Common Medical Issues.

Understanding how to respond quickly and efficiently to common medical issues can help prevent them from worsening into larger problems.

Cuts, scrapes, and wounds should be cleaned with antiseptic wipes or a saline solution and wrapped in sterile bandages to avoid infection. For deeper cuts, use a gauze pad and apply firm pressure to stop the bleeding before seeking medical attention.

To reduce swelling and irritation from insect bites and stings, apply antiseptic cream and anti-itch treatment. If you experience symptoms of an allergic reaction, such as hives or difficulty breathing, take an antihistamine and seek medical attention right away.

Symptoms of dehydration and heat exhaustion include dizziness, excessive thirst, and dark urine. Rest in the shade, hydrate with water or oral rehydration salts, and cool off with damp cloths. If heat stroke symptoms such as confusion or fainting appear, seek medical attention immediately.

Diarrhea and Stomach Issues: Take anti-diarrheal medication as needed and stay hydrated. Use oral rehydration solutions to replenish electrolytes that have been lost. If the symptoms persist or worsen, seek medical attention.

4. Identifying Severe Allergic Reactions (Anaphylaxis).
In the Amazon, you may come into contact with unfamiliar plants, insects, or foods that cause allergic reactions. Recognize the symptoms of anaphylaxis, which include:

- Swelling of the face, lips, and throat
- Having trouble breathing or wheezing
- Rapid heartbeat or dizziness.

173

- Severe rash or hives

Recommendation: If you have known severe allergies, always carry an epinephrine auto-injector and make sure your travel companions understand how to use it in an emergency. Even if your symptoms improve after using an auto-injector, seek medical attention right away.

5. Procedures for Snake and Insect Bites

While uncommon, bites from venomous snakes or dangerous insects can be fatal if not handled properly.

- *Keep Calm:* Panic can raise your heart rate and spread venom more quickly.
- *Immobilize the Affected Area:* Keep the affected limb still and at or below heart level.
- *Do Not Use Ice or Tourniquets:* These treatments can exacerbate the damage.
- *Seek Immediate Medical Attention:* Contact your guide or use your communication device to call for assistance as soon as possible.

Tip: Before your trip, become familiar with the types of venomous snakes and dangerous insects in the area. Your guide should carry or have access to a first-aid kit for snake bites.

6. Create an Emergency Evacuation Plan
If you are visiting the Amazon as part of a guided tour, your tour operator should have a clear emergency evacuation plan in place. Make sure you understand the plan's details, such as:

Nearest Medical Facility: Know where the closest hospital or clinic is and how to get there in an emergency.

Evacuation Transport: Learn about the transportation options available in the event of an emergency evacuation (e.g., boat, helicopter).

Carry a list of emergency contacts, including your guide's phone number, the emergency number for your lodge, and the nearest medical facilities.

7. Staying Prepared.
Take preventive measures throughout your journey. Carry your first aid kit, drink plenty of purified water, use insect repellent, and always follow your guide's advice. If you're traveling alone, consider hiring a local guide who knows the area and can help you in an emergency.

By following these first aid and emergency protocols, you can enjoy your Amazon adventure with confidence, knowing you are prepared for any unexpected situations.

Safety with Water and Food Consumption

Ensuring safe water and food consumption is crucial when visiting the Amazon, where tap water is typically not safe for drinking and local food preparation may differ from what travelers are accustomed to. Maintaining good practices when it comes to hydration and meals helps prevent common travel-related illnesses and ensures that your experience in the Amazon is enjoyable and worry-free. Here's how to stay healthy and vigilant about what you consume while exploring this unique environment.

1. Safe Drinking Water Practices
Tap water in the Amazon is unsafe to drink, and untreated water from rivers or lakes can contain pathogens that cause serious illnesses like giardiasis and other waterborne diseases. Here's how to keep your drinking water safe:

Use Bottled or Purified Water: Always choose bottled water from a reputable source. Before making a purchase, make sure the seal is intact. Alternatively, purified water from eco-lodges or tour operators is a safe option.

Bring a Portable Water Filter or Purification Tablets: If you plan to travel to remote areas where bottled water is not readily available, a portable water filter or purification tablets can be extremely useful. Water purifiers that use UV light technology can effectively eliminate the majority of bacteria and viruses.

Boil Water When Necessary: If purified water is unavailable, boiling water for at least one minute will kill most harmful organisms. Boil for longer at higher elevations to ensure safety.

Advice: Bring a reusable, BPA-free water bottle and refill it with safe water to stay hydrated on your trip. This reduces plastic waste and promotes eco-friendly travel practices.

2. Avoid Contaminated Water Sources

In tropical environments such as the Amazon, waterborne diseases can spread rapidly. To minimize risk:

Avoid Ice in Drinks: Unless you are certain that the ice was made with purified or bottled water, it is best to avoid it. Ice from tap water may contain the same pathogens that make tap water unsafe.

Avoid Unfamiliar Water Sources: Never drink directly from rivers, streams, or other natural water sources without first purifying the water, no matter how clean it appears.

Brush Your Teeth with Bottled Water: It's easy to forget, but even small amounts of contaminated water can be harmful. Brush your teeth with bottled or purified water.

Caution: Be wary of beverages containing local water or washed fruit juices that may have been prepared using tap water.

3. Selecting Safe Foods To Eat

The Amazon provides a diverse range of local cuisines, and trying new ones is part of the adventure. However, understanding food safety is critical to preventing foodborne illnesses:

Choose Cooked Foods: Hot, fully cooked foods are generally safe. Avoid dishes that have been at room temperature for an extended period of time or are only partially cooked.

176

Be Wary of Street Food: Street food can be a tempting way to sample local flavors, but it is critical to ensure that the vendor maintains good hygiene and that the food is freshly prepared and served hot.

Fruits with thick peels, such as bananas and oranges, are safer because the outer layer can be removed, reducing exposure to contaminants. Avoid pre-cut or washed fruits unless you know they were prepared with purified water.

Dairy Products: Exercise caution when handling dairy products, particularly those that have not been pasteurized. Stick to sealed and refrigerated items, or choose non-dairy alternatives whenever possible.

Tip: If you're unsure about the safety of a food source, err on the side of caution and stick to dishes that you know are prepared in sanitary conditions.

4. Prevention of Traveler's Diarrhea

Traveler's diarrhea is one of the most common illnesses among visitors to tropical countries. While not usually life-threatening, it can be extremely uncomfortable and disruptive. Here's how you can prevent it:

Maintain Good Hand Hygiene: Always wash your hands with soap and water before eating. If soap and water are not available, use a hand sanitizer containing at least 60% alcohol.

Carry antibacterial wipes to clean utensils, water bottle caps, and surfaces as needed.

Take Probiotics: Take probiotics a few days before your trip and during your stay. Probiotics help to balance your gut flora and reduce the likelihood of stomach problems.

Advice: Keep anti-diarrheal medication and oral rehydration salts in your first aid kit. Staying hydrated and taking these medications can effectively manage mild traveler's diarrhea symptoms.

5. What to Do If You Feel Ill

Despite your best efforts, illness can still occur. Knowing how to respond is critical for reducing discomfort and preventing dehydration.

Rehydrate Immediately: Dehydration can quickly worsen in a humid environment like the Amazon. Drink plenty of purified water and supplement with oral rehydration salts to replenish electrolytes.

Rest and Monitor Symptoms: If symptoms last longer than 48 hours, worsen, or include a high fever or severe abdominal pain, seek medical attention right away. Notify your guide or contact the nearest medical facility for assistance.

Dietary Adjustments: Eat bland, easy-to-digest foods like rice, bananas, and plain bread until your stomach settles.

Caution: If you suspect a more serious underlying illness or have symptoms such as blood in your stool or a high fever, do not take anti-diarrheal medication. In these situations, seek medical attention right away.

6. Foods to Enjoy and Avoid

Enjoying local cuisine is part of the Amazon experience. Accept foods that are known to be safe and nutritious, such as:

Stews and Grilled Meats: Traditional Amazonian stews and grilled fish or meats are frequently thoroughly cooked and served hot, reducing the possibility of contamination.

Cooked vegetables are generally safer than raw salads.

Exotic Fruits: Try fruits with thick peels, like mangoes, pineapples, and papayas, which you can peel yourself.

Foods To Avoid:

- Raw or undercooked seafood.
- Salads and unpeeled fruits washed with tap water
- Sauces or condiments that may have been left out for a long time

By adhering to these water and food safety practices, you can protect yourself from common travel-related illnesses and make your Amazon adventure as enjoyable and smooth as possible. Prioritizing health and hygiene will keep you energized and ready to experience everything this incredible region has to offer.

Staying Hydrated and Healthy in Humid Conditions

The Amazon Rainforest is known for its hot, humid climate, which can be challenging for travelers who aren't accustomed to such conditions. Maintaining proper hydration and taking steps to stay healthy is crucial for preventing dehydration, heat exhaustion, and other related issues. Here's how to stay hydrated and healthy while exploring the Amazon's unique environment.

1. Prioritize Hydration

The combination of high temperatures and humidity in the Amazon can result in rapid fluid loss via sweating. Even if you don't feel thirsty, you may still be losing significant amounts of water, so staying hydrated is critical.

Drink Plenty of Water: Aim to drink at least 2-3 liters (about 8-12 cups) of purified water per day, and increase this amount if you're participating in physically demanding activities like hiking or canoeing.

Avoid Dehydrating Drinks: Caffeinated or alcoholic beverages can cause fluid loss and dehydration. If you do consume these drinks, make sure to balance them out with plenty of water.

Bring a high-quality, BPA-free reusable water bottle that you can refill frequently with purified water. Some eco-lodges and guided tours have safe drinking water stations, making it easy to stay hydrated and reduce plastic waste.

Tip: Add a pinch of salt or electrolyte tablets to your water to help maintain electrolyte balance, especially after strenuous exercise.

2. Recognize the signs of dehydration.

Dehydration can occur quickly, especially in the Amazon's humid climate, so it's critical to recognize early warning signs and take action.

- Mild Signs: Thirst, dry mouth, and dark urine.
- Moderate signs include dizziness, fatigue, headaches, and decreased urine output.
- Severe symptoms include rapid heartbeat, confusion, or fainting. These require immediate care and hydration with electrolyte solutions or oral rehydration salts.

Check the color of your urine to see how well you're hydrated. Pale or light-yellow urine indicates adequate hydration, whereas darker shades indicate a need for additional fluids.

3. Choose Hydrating Foods.
In addition to drinking water, eating foods high in water content can help you stay hydrated and provide essential nutrients.

Fruits: Watermelon, oranges, pineapples, and papayas are excellent sources of hydration as well as essential vitamins and minerals.

Vegetables: Cucumbers, tomatoes, and leafy greens are high in water and help hydrate.

Soups and Stews: Local Amazonian stews can help you stay hydrated and nourished. Choose broths made with safe, purified water and fresh ingredients.

Carry snack packs containing dried fruits and nuts. While they do not hydrate you, they do provide quick energy to help you maintain your stamina in the humid climate.

4. Dress smartly to stay cool.

Wearing the appropriate clothing can have a significant impact on your comfort and hydration levels in a humid environment.

Lightweight, Breathable Fabrics: Wear clothing made of moisture-wicking materials, which allow your skin to breathe and help manage sweat. Ideal fabrics include cotton and moisture-wicking synthetic blends.

Wear loose-fitting clothes to promote airflow and help keep your body temperature low.

Wide-Brimmed Hat and Sunglasses: A wide-brimmed hat protects your face and neck from the sun and reduces heat absorption. Polarized sunglasses protect your eyes from glare.

Caution: Avoid wearing heavy or dark clothing, as they can absorb heat and cause overheating. Also, avoid non-breathable synthetic fabrics, which can trap heat and moisture.

5. Rest frequently and find shade.
The Amazon can be physically demanding, and resting in shaded areas helps your body recover and stay hydrated.

Take Regular Breaks: Whether you're on a guided hike, canoeing, or exploring a nearby village, stop every 30-45 minutes to rest and drink water.

Seek Natural Shade: Look for shaded areas under trees or use temporary shelters if you're in an open space. Resting in the shade allows your body to cool down and lowers the risk of overheating.

To avoid peak heat, plan your more strenuous activities for cooler times of day, such as early mornings or late afternoons.

6. Managing Humidity and Sweat
High humidity can cause you to sweat profusely even when you're not working out. If not properly managed, this sweat can cause dehydration, heat rash, and fungal infections.

Sweat-Absorbing Accessories: Carry a small towel or wear a sweatband to absorb excess moisture and keep sweat from getting into your eyes.

Stay Dry When Possible: Change into dry clothes after excessive sweating or being caught in the rain to avoid skin irritation and reduce the risk of fungal infections.

Apply Talcum Powder or Anti-Chafing Cream: These products can help reduce skin irritation and chafing, particularly in areas prone to friction.

7. Practice good hygiene.

Maintaining good hygiene helps to prevent the spread of bacteria and illnesses, which are exacerbated by humid conditions.

Wash Your Hands Frequently: Use soap and purified water, or carry hand sanitizer containing at least 60% alcohol.

Keep Hydration Supplies Clean: To avoid contamination, clean your water bottle and any other drinking water containers on a regular basis.

Caution: If you begin to feel unwell, such as persistent headaches, dizziness, or confusion, seek medical attention right away because these could be symptoms of dehydration or heat exhaustion.

Staying hydrated and healthy in the Amazon's humid climate necessitates careful planning and constant vigilance. By following these guidelines, you'll be better prepared to deal with the challenging conditions while enjoying everything the Amazon has to offer.

Access to Medical Facilities and Support

Access to medical facilities and support in the Amazon can vary greatly depending on your location. Major cities and towns that serve as gateways to the Amazon, such as Manaus in Brazil, Iquitos in Peru, and Leticia in Colombia, often have hospitals or medical clinics with a reasonable level of care. However, once you venture deeper into the rainforest, access to healthcare can become limited or non-existent. Understanding what medical facilities are available and how to seek support is vital for ensuring your safety during your journey.

1. Medical Facilities in Gateway Cities

Larger cities and towns that serve as entry points to the Amazon have hospitals and clinics that provide a variety of medical services. These facilities may include English-speaking doctors, modern equipment, and pharmacies stocked with necessary medications.

Manaus, Brazil: As the Amazon's largest city, Manaus has a number of hospitals and clinics, including private facilities that provide higher levels of care. Travelers can often reach out to specialists and emergency services for serious medical concerns.

Iquitos, Peru: While Iquitos has fewer resources than Manaus, it does have several hospitals and clinics that serve travelers. Private clinics may offer better service with shorter wait times.

Leticia, Colombia: Leticia has basic healthcare facilities and clinics that can treat minor injuries and diseases. For more serious medical conditions, evacuation to larger Colombian cities or neighboring countries may be required.

Recommendation: Before traveling, look into the healthcare options available in the cities or towns where your tour begins and ends. This knowledge can help you plan and respond quickly in the event of a medical emergency.

2. Medical Support for Remote Areas

Access to healthcare becomes limited as you travel further into the Amazon, with medical facilities sometimes being hours or even days away. Here are some key considerations for staying prepared:

Travel with a Guide: Guided tours frequently include a local guide who is trained in basic first aid and can help coordinate emergency assistance. Guides are also familiar with the area and can help you find local healthcare providers or arrange transportation to the nearest medical facility.

Emergency Evacuation Plans: Make sure your tour operator has a clear emergency evacuation plan in place. This plan should specify how you will be transported to the nearest hospital or medical center in the event of a serious health emergency. Some tour operators collaborate with private companies that provide helicopter or speedboat services for emergency medical evacuation.

First Aid Kits: While you should always bring your own well-stocked first aid kit, reputable tour operators will often provide an advanced medical kit and basic first aid supplies. Inquire with your operator about the medical supplies they have and whether any of the guides have received CPR and advanced first aid training.

Advice: If you have a chronic medical condition, bring a letter from your doctor explaining your condition, the medications you need, and any potential complications. This information is useful if you need to communicate with a medical professional who may not be fluent in your language.

3. Medical insurance and emergency coverage.

Travel insurance that covers medical emergencies, including medical evacuation, is required when visiting the Amazon. Medical evacuations can be expensive, so having insurance to cover these costs will give you peace of mind.

Check Your Coverage: Make sure your travel insurance policy specifically covers the activities you intend to participate in, such as hiking, canoeing, or wildlife safaris. Confirm that it includes emergency medical evacuation to a higher-level medical facility, if necessary.

Medical Air Evacuation Services: Some travelers choose additional coverage that includes access to private air ambulance services. This is especially useful in remote areas of the Amazon, where reaching a medical facility by land or river can take hours.

Caution: Not all standard travel insurance policies cover medical evacuation or adventure activities, so thoroughly review your policy and upgrade as needed.

4. Pharmacies and Medicine Availability

Access to pharmacies and medications varies greatly depending on where you are. Pharmacies are available and well-stocked with basic medicines in larger towns and gateway cities, but the selection may be limited in rural areas.

Bring Essential Medications: Make sure you have a good supply of any prescription medications you require, as well as over-the-counter medications for common ailments like allergies, pain, stomach discomfort, or fever.

Keep Medications Properly Stored: Some medications may be affected by the Amazon's humid climate. Keep them in waterproof, airtight containers and in a cool, shaded area of your travel bag.

Know the Generic Names: If you run out of a medication or need to replace it, knowing its generic name (rather than just the brand name) can be useful when speaking with a pharmacist.

5. What to do in case of emergency

Knowing how to act during a medical emergency is critical:

Notify Your Guide: If you or anyone in your group has a medical emergency, notify your guide immediately. Guides can initiate emergency protocols and coordinate with local services to provide assistance.

Use Communication Devices: In remote areas where cell service is unreliable, contact emergency services or your tour operator via satellite phone or emergency radio.

Follow First Aid Protocols: Keep the patient as stable as possible until further assistance arrives. This includes keeping them hydrated, preventing shock, and providing first aid for any wounds or injuries.

6. Local health considerations

Some remote villages may have basic health outposts, but they frequently offer limited services. They can provide initial care for minor injuries and illnesses, but they are not prepared to handle serious medical conditions.

Participate in Community Health Initiatives: Some travelers choose to contribute to or volunteer for local health initiatives that benefit Amazonian communities. This can be a way to give back to the community and help improve medical infrastructure.

Recommendation: If you plan on volunteering or staying in a village for an extended period of time, check out the local medical resources and consider bringing additional medical supplies that will benefit both you and the community.

Access to medical facilities and support in the Amazon requires careful planning and awareness of your surroundings. While exploring this remarkable and challenging region, you can significantly improve your safety and well-being by planning ahead of time, carrying essential supplies, and staying informed about emergency protocols.

CHAPTER 10

ITINERARIES AND MUST-SEE DESTINATIONS ALONG THE AMAZON

Popular Ports and Stops on the Amazon River

The Amazon River is not just a lifeline for the rainforest; it's a gateway to experiencing the rich culture, history, and biodiversity of the region. Travelers venturing on an Amazon River cruise or exploring by other means will find a variety of popular ports and stops that showcase the unique essence of this incredible region. Here's a detailed guide to some of the most notable destinations along the Amazon River, complete with recommendations, key highlights, and advice for making the most of each visit.

1. Manaus, Brazil – The Gateway to the Amazon

Manaus is the largest city on the Amazon River and a popular port for river cruises and expeditions. Known as the "Gateway to the Amazon," this bustling metropolis is rich in history and culture, blending modernity with rainforest traditions.

Key attractions include the iconic Teatro Amazonas, an opera house that exemplifies the grandeur of the city's rubber boom era, and the Meeting of the Waters, where the dark Rio Negro and the sandy-colored Amazon River run side by side for several miles without mixing.

Markets and Cuisine: Stop by the Adolpho Lisboa Municipal Market for a taste of local flavors, fresh produce, and exotic Amazonian fish like tambaqui and pirarucu.

Recommendations: Spend at least a day exploring Manaus before starting your river journey. Join a guided tour to learn about the city's history and how to safely navigate the region.

Advice: Manaus can be hot and humid all year, so wear lightweight, breathable clothing and drink plenty of water. Also, be wary of pickpockets in congested market areas.

2. Iquitos, Peru: The Largest City Not Accessible by Road

Iquitos is the world's largest city without a road, accessible only by air or river. This distinguishing feature makes it an appealing and remote starting point for Amazon adventures in Peru. Iquitos is a popular destination for exploring the Peruvian Amazon, with a vibrant culture and fascinating wildlife experiences.

Key attractions include the Belén Floating Market, which features floating houses and a diverse range of Amazonian goods, and the Pilpintuwasi Butterfly Farm, which also serves as an animal rescue center.

Wildlife Excursions: Iquitos is an excellent starting point for wildlife tours, with chances to see pink river dolphins, sloths, and a variety of monkey species.

Cultural Highlights: Visit the Casa de Fierro (Iron House), a one-of-a-kind structure reportedly designed by Gustave Eiffel that commemorates the city's connection to the rubber boom era.

Join a guided excursion into the Pacaya-Samiria National Reserve, one of Peru's largest protected areas, where you can see pristine rainforest ecosystems and a variety of wildlife.

3. Santarém, Brazil: The Confluence of Rivers

Santarém is located at the confluence of the Tapajós and Amazon rivers, resulting in a stunning visual display known as the "Meeting of the Waters." This port city is well-known for its blend of indigenous and colonial history, making it an excellent destination for those looking for cultural immersion.

Alter do Chão village, known as the "Caribbean of the Amazon," offers stunning white-sand river beaches ideal for relaxation. The João Fona Cultural Center explores local history and indigenous artifacts.

Natural Wonders: The nearby Tapajós National Forest is a nature lover's paradise, offering a variety of activities such as hiking, birdwatching, and boat tours.

Culinary Experience: Try traditional Amazonian dishes like piracuí, made from ground fish.

Alter do Chão's beaches are seasonal, appearing during the dry months (August-November). Plan your trip accordingly to enjoy these natural wonders.

4. Leticia, Colombia: The Tricultural Border Town.

Leticia is a small but vibrant town located on the border of Colombia, Peru, and Brazil. It's an excellent choice for travelers looking to experience a variety of cultures while exploring the Amazon from a less touristy perspective.

Key attractions include the Amazonian Manatee Rescue Center, which rehabilitates manatees and educates visitors about conservation, and the Parque Santander, which is famous for its nightly spectacle of thousands of parrots returning to roost.

Cultural Highlights: Visit the tricultural market, where vendors from Colombia, Peru, and Brazil sell a variety of goods and foods, creating a rich cultural blend unique to the region.

Excursions: Leticia is the gateway to Amacayacu National Park, where you can hike, canoe, and enjoy the rainforest's incredible biodiversity.

Recommendation: Set aside time to visit Tabatinga, a neighboring Brazilian town, to see how borders blend seamlessly in this region. Keep your passport handy, as crossing borders is common and mostly informal, but identification may be required.

5. Parintins, Brazil: Home of the Boi-Bumbá Festival.

Parintins is best known for its vibrant Boi-Bumbá Festival, which takes place every June and celebrates Amazonian folklore. It is one of Brazil's most colorful and extravagant festivals, second only to Rio Carnival.

Key Attractions: If you're visiting during the festival, the Bumbódromo stadium is the place to be. The competition between the "Caprichoso" and "Garantido" teams features elaborate performances, music, and costumes.

Cultural Experience: In addition to the festival, Parintins provides insight into the indigenous and Afro-Brazilian traditions that are central to local culture.

Local Artisans: The city is well-known for its handmade crafts and souvenirs featuring Amazonian themes, making it an excellent place to buy mementos.

Caution: Parintins can get very crowded during the Boi-Bumbá Festival. If you intend to visit during this time, make your reservations and tickets well in advance.

6. Belém, Brazil—The Gateway to the Amazon Delta

Belém is the main city at the mouth of the Amazon River, where it meets the Atlantic Ocean. This bustling port city is well-known for its colonial architecture, cultural attractions, and the Ver-o-Peso Market, which is one of Latin America's largest outdoor markets.

Key attractions include the Forte do Presépio and the Museu Paraense Emílio Goeldi, which exhibit Amazonian wildlife and indigenous artifacts.

Belém is known for its culinary delights, such as açaí, tacacá, and Amazonian flavors. It's a must-see for foodies looking to sample authentic Amazonian cuisine.

Natural Excursions: Belém serves as a jumping off point for exploring Marajó Island, which is known for its unique blend of Amazonian and Atlantic ecosystems, including water buffalo herds and traditional pottery.

The heat and humidity in Belém can be intense, so plan to visit outdoor markets and attractions early in the morning or late afternoon. Try the local açaí, which is thicker and richer than that found elsewhere.

When planning your Amazon itinerary, keep in mind the unique offerings of each port and stop. Whether you're drawn to the cultural vibrancy of festivals, the tranquil beauty of river beaches, or the deep exploration of wildlife reserves, each Amazon River destination has its own unique appeal. Prioritize the experiences that are relevant to your interests, and plan your trip with local guides to ensure safe and enriching interactions.

Highlights of Iquitos, Manaus, Leticia, and Beyond

Exploring the Amazon River means delving into its most significant cities and towns, each offering its own unique blend of culture, history, and natural wonders. Iquitos, Manaus, and Leticia are key destinations that provide travelers with access to some of the most immersive experiences in the Amazon. Here's a detailed look at what makes these places special and what you shouldn't miss while visiting.

1. Iquitos, Peru – The Enigmatic Gateway to the Peruvian Amazon

Iquitos, the world's largest city that cannot be reached by road, is both mysterious and lively. This vibrant city is located on the banks of the Amazon River and serves as a starting point for numerous jungle expeditions and river cruises.

Belén Market and Floating District: One of Iquitos' most striking features is the Belén Market, a sprawling open-air market that sells everything from Amazonian fruits to exotic herbs and traditional medicine. The Belén Floating District is a fascinating neighborhood where houses rise and fall with the water levels, providing an eye-opening look at how locals adapt to the river's rhythms.

Manatee Rescue Center: For an enriching conservation experience, go to the Amazonian Manatee Rescue Center and learn about efforts to rehabilitate orphaned and injured manatees.

Wildlife and Nature Reserves: Iquitos is an excellent starting point for exploring nearby nature reserves such as the Pacaya-Samiria National Reserve, which offers pristine rainforest and encounters with pink river dolphins, sloths, monkeys, and a variety of bird species.

Recommendation: Take a guided day trip or multi-day excursion to the Pacaya-Samiria Reserve to fully appreciate Amazon biodiversity. For those interested in ethnobotany, local guides can show you medicinal plants and traditional healing practices.

Advice: Be cautious when visiting Belén Market, as it can get crowded and pickpocketing is common. Always be aware of your surroundings and keep your belongings safe.

2. Manaus, Brazil—The Heart of the Amazon Rainforest
Manaus is the bustling capital of the Amazonas state and the primary entry point for those visiting the Brazilian Amazon. It is known for its rich history, cultural landmarks, and as a starting point for some of the most popular Amazonian tours.

Teatro Amazonas: No trip to Manaus is complete without visiting the Teatro Amazonas, an opulent opera house constructed during the rubber boom. Its lavish architecture and interior, complete with imported European materials, reflect the city's prosperous past.

Meeting of the Waters: One of Manaus' natural wonders is the Meeting of the Waters, where the dark Rio Negro and the sandy Amazon River flow for miles without mixing. The striking color contrast is caused by differences in temperature, speed, and sediment content between the two rivers.

Museums and Cultural Centers: The Museu do Seringal (Rubber Museum) explores the history of rubber extraction and its impact on the region's economy and indigenous communities.

Eco-Lodges and Wildlife Tours: Manaus is a hub for river cruises and eco-lodges that provide immersive experiences such as jungle hikes, piranha fishing, and night tours to see nocturnal wildlife.

Recommendation: For a more intimate wildlife experience, stay at an eco-lodge a few hours from Manaus. These lodges offer guided tours that take you deeper into the rainforest, away from the city's hustle and bustle.

Caution: Manaus can be extremely hot and humid, so wear light, breathable clothing and use insect repellent on a regular basis.

3. Leticia, Colombia: A Tricultural Hub on the Amazon.

Leticia is a charming town located at the crossroads of Colombia, Peru, and Brazil, making it an ideal destination for travelers seeking a cultural fusion. Despite its small size, Leticia is full of experiences and serves as an excellent base for exploring the Colombian Amazon.

Parque Santander: This park is famous for the daily sight of thousands of parrots returning to roost at sunset. The sight and sound of these birds is breathtaking and a must-see for nature lovers.

The Amazonian Manatee Rescue Center in Leticia, like the one in Iquitos, is dedicated to conservation and education.

Local Markets: Leticia's markets feature a unique blend of Colombian, Peruvian, and Brazilian products. You can find Amazonian delicacies, exotic fruits, and local crafts here.

River Excursions: From Leticia, visitors can take river tours to nearby reserves such as Amacayacu National Park, which is known for its rich biodiversity and opportunities for birdwatching, trekking, and meeting indigenous people.

Recommendation: Visit the nearby town of Tabatinga, Brazil, which is only a short walk from Leticia, to witness the seamless cultural blending at the border. Remember to bring your passport, as the crossing between these towns, while informal, may require identification.

Leticia has a relaxed atmosphere, but the heat and humidity can be intense. Stay hydrated, wear sunscreen, and take breaks in the shade as needed.

4. Beyond These Cities: Hidden Gems and Lesser-Known Stops.

While Iquitos, Manaus, and Leticia are the most popular destinations, the Amazon has a plethora of smaller towns and villages that provide more secluded and distinct experiences.

Alter do Chão, also known as the "Caribbean of the Amazon," is a village in Brazil known for its white-sand river beaches and clear waters. The best time to visit is in the dry season (August to November), when the beaches are at their best.

Santander (Peru): This quiet town offers a slower pace and the opportunity to immerse yourself in local culture. Visitors can explore local craft workshops, meet indigenous artisans, and learn about generations-old techniques.

Moyobamba (Peru): Known as the "City of Orchids," Moyobamba is a botanical wonderland that is ideal for nature lovers and orchid enthusiasts.

Pucallpa (Peru): A port city that serves as a springboard for further Amazon exploration. It is famous for its thriving arts scene and indigenous Shipibo-Konibo artisans who make intricate textiles and crafts.

Recommendation: For a truly unique experience, visit community-led tourism projects. These offer an opportunity to learn about local traditions, give back to the community, and experience the Amazon in a more sustainable and responsible way.

Caution: The further you travel from major cities, the fewer amenities and medical facilities are available. Always travel with a well-stocked first-aid kit and be familiar with emergency procedures.

Exploring Iquitos, Manaus, Leticia, and other Amazon destinations provides a diverse, dynamic, and deeply rooted cultural and natural experience. Whether you're drawn to the architectural splendor of Manaus, the remote charm of Iquitos, the multicultural blend of Leticia, or the hidden treasures of smaller communities, each Amazon stop offers a journey of discovery and awe.

Unique Sites: Meeting of the Waters, Pink River Dolphins

The Amazon River is filled with breathtaking natural phenomena, but two of the most captivating and unique experiences are witnessing the Meeting of the Waters and encountering the mystical pink river dolphins. Both of these attractions offer visitors an unparalleled glimpse into the natural wonders of the Amazon and provide unforgettable memories. Here's an in-depth look at these unique sites and how to experience them to the fullest.

1. The Meeting of the Waters (Encontro das Águas)

The Meeting of the Waters is a natural phenomenon that occurs just outside the city of Manaus, Brazil. The dark waters of the Rio Negro and the sandy-colored waters of the Solimões River (upper Amazon) flow side by side without mixing for approximately 6 kilometers. The stark contrast between the two rivers creates a clear visual line that captivates visitors, making this a must-see stop on any Amazon itinerary.

Why It Happens: The Rio Negro and Solimões Rivers differ significantly in temperature, speed, and density. The Rio Negro flows at a slower rate of about 2 km/h, is warmer (with temperatures around 28°C/82°F), and contains a high concentration of organic material, giving it a dark, almost black appearance. The Solimões River flows faster at 4-6 km/h, is cooler (approximately 22°C/72°F), and contains silt and sediment, resulting in its lighter, muddy color.

How to Experience It: The best way to see this natural wonder is on a boat tour. Various river tours and day cruises departing from Manaus provide opportunities to see the Meeting of the Waters up close, allowing you to observe the unique contrast and even touch the water to feel the temperature difference.

Guided Tours: Many tours include knowledgeable guides who can explain the phenomenon's scientific and cultural significance while also pointing out other interesting aspects of the surrounding environment, such as bird species and riverside vegetation.

Photography Tip: The best time to photograph this spectacle is in the morning or late afternoon, when the light reflects beautifully on the water. Bring a camera with a good zoom lens to capture the clear distinction between the two rivers.

While most boat tours are safe and run by reputable operators, always read reviews and select a company that values safety and sustainability. Wearing a hat, applying sunscreen, and staying hydrated are essential because you will be exposed to the sun during the boat trip.

2. Pink River Dolphins (Boto).

The pink river dolphin, also known as Inia geoffrensis, is one of the Amazon's most enchanting and mysterious creatures. These dolphins are known not only for their distinctive pinkish color, but also for their unique adaptations to river life. Sightings of these dolphins are considered the highlight of any Amazon adventure.

Physical characteristics and adaptations: Pink river dolphins can grow to be 2.5 meters (8 feet) long and weigh up to 185 kilograms (408 pounds). They are born gray and gradually develop pink coloration, which is more noticeable in males and can range from a subtle blush to a vibrant pink. This distinct color is thought to be influenced by blood capillaries near the surface of the skin. Unlike their oceanic counterparts, pink river dolphins have flexible necks that allow them to easily navigate flooded forests and narrow waterways.

Behavior and Social Structure: These dolphins are known for their playful and curious nature, and they frequently interact with humans on guided tours. Pink river dolphins are more solitary than bottlenose dolphins, though they can be seen swimming in pairs or small groups. They use echolocation to navigate the Amazon's murky waters and find prey such as fish, crustaceans, and small turtles.

Pink river dolphins can be found throughout the Amazon Basin, but popular spots for sightings include the Pacaya-Samiria National Reserve in Peru, the Mamiráua Reserve in Brazil, and near the town of Leticia in Colombia. Dolphin encounter tours are frequently held in the early morning or late afternoon, when dolphins are at their most active.

Conservation Concerns: The pink river dolphin is listed as endangered due to threats such as habitat destruction, pollution, and accidental entanglement in fishing nets. Some tour operators collaborate with conservation projects to educate visitors about the importance of protecting these incredible creatures and their habitats.

Recommendation: Select tours that promote ethical wildlife viewing. Ensure that operators follow responsible practices, such as keeping a respectful distance and avoiding activities that interfere with the dolphins' natural behavior. Never feed or touch wild dolphins, as this can harm them and disrupt their natural behavior.

Respectful interaction with wildlife.

- To help protect pink river dolphins and other wildlife, please follow these guidelines:

- Maintain a Safe Distance: Keep a respectful distance from dolphins and other wildlife to avoid disrupting their natural behaviors.
- *Avoid Feeding:* Feeding wild dolphins or other animals can disrupt their natural feeding habits and put them in danger if they learn to associate humans with food.
- *Choose Responsible Tour Operators:* Look for tour companies that follow strict wildlife regulations and promote conservation efforts. Operators should prioritize the well-being of wildlife over profit and be open about their practices.

Advice: Bring binoculars for better dolphin watching, as they can sometimes be seen from a distance, and be prepared to wait. Wildlife spotting can be unpredictable, so make room in your schedule to increase your chances of seeing these creatures.

Cultural Significance

The pink river dolphin is revered in the folklore of many Amazonian cultures. They are frequently depicted in stories as mystical beings capable of transforming into humans and appearing on shore during festivals and celebrations. These legends add to the strong bond that many locals have with dolphins and the river itself. Respect for these beliefs is essential when interacting with local guides or visiting indigenous villages.

While witnessing the Meeting of the Waters and encountering pink river dolphins are memorable experiences, both should be approached with respect and responsibility. By choosing sustainable tours and practicing mindful observation, you can help to preserve these natural wonders for future generations.

Suggested Day Trips and Local Guided Tours

Day trips and guided tours are essential for making the most of your Amazon River experience. These excursions provide an immersive way to explore the natural beauty, culture, and biodiversity of the region, often led by local experts who offer invaluable knowledge about the rainforest and its inhabitants. Here are some of the best day trips and guided tours to consider, each designed to help you appreciate the Amazon's complexity and splendor.

1. Wildlife and Birdwatching Tours

The Amazon is home to some of the world's most diverse and distinctive wildlife. Day trips focused on wildlife and birdwatching allow visitors to see creatures that may not be seen anywhere else on earth.

Highlights include spotted toucans, scarlet macaws, hoatzins, and harpy eagles, as well as a variety of monkey, sloth, and reptile species. Early morning tours often provide the best opportunity to observe birds and other wildlife at their most active.

Recommended Locations: The Pacaya-Samiria National Reserve in Peru, the Mamirauá Sustainable Development Reserve in Brazil, and the Yasuni National Park in Ecuador are excellent places to observe wildlife.

Guides: Choose tours led by local naturalists or biologists with extensive knowledge of the region's fauna. They can provide information about animal behavior, migration patterns, and conservation efforts.

Bring binoculars and a camera with a zoom lens for improved viewing and photography. Early morning tours frequently feature cooler temperatures and increased wildlife activity, making them ideal for these excursions.

Advice: Avoid using flash photography because it can disturb wildlife and disrupt their natural behaviors. Respect the guide's instructions for keeping a safe distance from animals to ensure both your safety and the wildlife's well-being.

2. Riverboat and Canoe Tours.

Exploring the Amazon from the water provides a unique perspective on the river's ecosystem. Riverboat and canoe tours take you through narrow tributaries, flooded forests, and secluded lakes that larger boats cannot navigate.

Highlights: These tours allow you to see pink river dolphins, caimans, giant otters, and a variety of aquatic birds. Canoe tours are ideal for silently gliding through smaller, quieter waterways that provide more intimate wildlife encounters.

Best Times: Water levels in the Amazon vary seasonally. The wet season (December to May) allows canoes to enter flooded forest areas, whereas the dry season (June to November) may limit access but provide better opportunities to explore riverbanks and spot wildlife.

Guides: Choose experienced local guides who know how to navigate the waterways and spot wildlife. Their knowledge can significantly impact what you see and learn during your trip.

Tip: Wear a hat, use sunscreen, and bring insect repellent. Water reflects sunlight, increasing your exposure to UV rays, and mosquitoes are more active near water.

Caution: Consult your tour operator about safety protocols and life jackets. Canoe tours, particularly in deeper or faster-moving water, necessitate adequate safety precautions.

3. Indigenous Community Visits
Visiting indigenous communities provides an authentic view of the Amazon's cultural diversity and allows visitors to learn from those who have coexisted with the rainforest for generations.

Highlights: Enjoy traditional dances, crafts, and stories told by community elders. Some tours may include workshops on how to use local plants for medicinal purposes or a sample of indigenous cuisine.

Recommended Locations: Many communities near Iquitos, Manaus, and Leticia welcome visitors with guided tours that benefit their economy and cultural preservation. Ensure that the tour is booked through reputable operators who engage in ethical and respectful behavior.

Guides: Local guides who are members of or have close connections to the communities can provide valuable context and serve as a liaison between visitors and residents.

Tip: To show appreciation, bring a small, respectful gift such as school supplies or non-perishable food items, but first consult with your guide to determine what is appropriate.

Advice: Always seek permission before photographing people or their homes. Be open-minded, respectful, and avoid imposing your own cultural beliefs.

4. Jungle Trekking and Nightwalks
Jungle treks and night walks offer a closer look at the Amazon's lush ecosystem. Day treks take you deep into the rainforest to learn about the diverse flora and fauna, whereas night walks reveal nocturnal creatures and jungle sounds that are typically hidden during the day.

Highlights include poison dart frogs, gigantic insects, snakes, and caimans' glowing eyes. Listen to the distinctive calls of nocturnal birds and observe the subtle movements of night-active mammals.

Best Practices: To avoid startling animals, wear long sleeves and insect repellent-treated pants and bring a headlamp or flashlight with a red light.

Expert guides can identify different plants and animals, explaining their roles in the ecosystem and how they are used in local traditions. They can also keep you safe by navigating trails that may contain hidden roots, sharp plants, or steep inclines.

Tip: Bring a lightweight rain poncho and waterproof footwear, as sudden rain is common even during the dry season. A trekking pole can be useful for maintaining balance on uneven terrain.

Caution: Do not touch plants or animals without consulting your expert, as some can be toxic or dangerous. Always stick with the group to avoid getting lost in the dense forest.

5. Medicinal Plant Tours

These specialized tours offer an in-depth look at the Amazon's vast array of medicinal plants and the extensive knowledge that local and indigenous communities have about their applications.

Highlights: Discover the traditional uses for plants like ayahuasca, cat's claw, and sangre de drago (dragon's blood). Expert guides, often from indigenous communities, explain how plants are used for healing, health maintenance, and spiritual practices.

Best Locations: Medicinal plant tours are popular in the areas surrounding Iquitos and Manaus, where local healers and botanists frequently lead the tours.

Tip: Take notes or request printed information if available. Many guides will be happy to share basic recipes or treatments discussed during the tour.

Advice: Never consume or use any plant-based remedy without first consulting an expert. The potency and effects of Amazonian plants can be very strong, so proceed with caution.

6. Eco-Lodge Day Excursions.

Eco-lodges provide day trips that include activities such as wildlife watching, guided nature hikes, and canoe trips for those seeking a balance of comfort and adventure. Eco-lodges are typically designed to blend into the environment while providing eco-friendly amenities.

Highlights: Day excursions frequently include meals made with locally sourced ingredients, opportunities to spot wildlife from observation towers, and walks that focus on specific aspects of the rainforest, such as birdwatching or plant identification.

Sustainability: Look for eco-lodges that have been certified for their sustainable practices and conservation efforts. Many lodges work with the local community to promote cultural and environmental education.

Recommendation: Look for lodges that provide small group tours for a more personalized experience and reduced environmental impact.

Final Tip: Whatever type of tour you choose, make sure to travel with an open mind, patience, and a sense of respect. The Amazon is a complex and fragile ecosystem, and responsible travel helps to preserve its wonders for future generations.

Made in the USA
Las Vegas, NV
31 January 2025

17275815R00115